ARTIFICIAL PRESENCE

Cultural Memory
in
the
Present

Mieke Bal and Hent de Vries, Editors

ARTIFICIAL PRESENCE

Philosophical Studies in Image Theory

Lambert Wiesing

Translated by Nils F. Schott

STANFORD UNIVERSITY PRESS

STANFORD, CALIFORNIA

Stanford University Press
Stanford, California

Artificial Presence: Philosophical Studies in Image Theory was originally published in
German under the title *Artifizielle Präsenz: Studien zur Philosophie des Bildes*
© Suhrkamp Verlag Frankfurt am Main, 2005.

The translation of this work was supported by a grant from the Goethe-Institut
which is funded by the German Ministry of Foreign Affairs.

Library of Congress Cataloging-in-Publication Data

Wiesing, Lambert.
   [Artifizielle Präsenz. English]
   Artificial presence : philosophical studies in image theory / Lambert Wiesing ;
translated by Nils F. Schott.
      p.   cm. — (Cultural memory in the present)
   "Originally published in German in 2005 under the title Artifizielle Präsenz:
Studien zur Philosophie des Bildes."
   Includes bibliographical references.
   ISBN 978-0-8047-5940-3 (cloth : alk. paper)
   ISBN 978-0-8047-5941-0 (pbk. : alk. paper)
   1. Image (Philosophy)   2. Art—Philosophy.   I. Title.   II. Series: Cultural
memory in the present.
B105.I47W5413   2010
111'.85—dc22
                                                      2009018393

Contents

Preface

The studies collected in this volume trace a conceptual field. The concept of the image is at their center. Each of the eight studies describes the relation of this concept to an adjacent concept. The conceptual field thematized here includes the concepts of the sign, of abstract photography, of the window, of virtual reality and immersion, of mimesis, and of the medium. However heterogeneous the phenomena addressed might be, the thesis defended in all of the studies remains no less unified. Only if the artificial presence of the objects visible in images is understood as the specific characteristic of each and every image do the disciplines of image studies work with a concept of the image that is able to capture both the irreplaceable capacity of the image and its resulting relevance to the human. Human beings are convinced that they can see something in an image even though, at the same time, they are certain that this something is not really, but only artificially, present. That is the topic of this book, the phenomenon that the image opens up a view on a reality liberated from the constraints of physics.

For the most part these essays and lectures, written between 2000 and 2004, are published here for the first time; essays published previously have been revised. In their elaboration I was fortunate to receive help in many ways, and I would therefore like to thank Stefan Matuschek, Stephan Günzel, Michael Albert Islinger, Grit Hammer, Sandra Gadinger, Silvia Seja, Iris Därmann, Manfred Sommer, Ralph Behrwald, Gottfried Jäger, Thomas Rolf, Wolfgang Kienzler, and Klaus Rehkämper.

L.W.
Sendenhorst, June 2004

A German book's translation into English is always a particularly pleasant development for its author. All of a sudden the possibility opens up that a significantly larger readership will receive the author's reflections. I am glad that, thanks to this translation, this is true for my phenomenology of artificial presence as well. Hence it is important to me to express my thanks for the support the realization of this translation has received. Thanks are due especially to Hans Ulrich Gumbrecht, who, very early and very enthusiastically, supported this project. I am glad that in Nils F. Schott my book has found a translator who has taken up even the least of my suggestions and always knew how to implement them convincingly. I am grateful for the suggestions I received from Dawn Phillips, Jens Bonnemann, and Nico Brömßer in discussions of the final version. The translation project received a driving force, and I received particularly helpful contacts, in Emily-Jane Cohen and Sarah Crane Newman at Stanford University Press. It was Ms. Cohen, too, who supported the idea to publish the American edition, unlike the German original, with several illustrations—indeed a rewarding addition, whose realization is indebted to the support of Gottfried Jäger.

L.W.
Sendenhorst, June 2009

Translator's Note

The translation of *Artificial Presence* has been an enjoyable endeavor for me, and I hope this volume will succeed in making Lambert Wiesing's work accessible to an English-speaking audience. Given the richness of the idioms and technical vocabulary employed by the author, occasional clarifications in square brackets and footnotes, as well as a glossary of key terms, will, I trust, prove helpful. Published translations of all texts quoted have been reviewed and, if necessary, modified in accordance with their employment in the German edition of *Artificial Presence*. All other translations are mine.

My thanks go to the editors at Stanford University Press, Emily-Jane Cohen, Sarah Crane Newman, Tim Roberts, and Joe Abbott, for the patience and promptness with which they have supported this project throughout. Special thanks are due to the series editors, Hent de Vries and Mieke Bal. Lambert Wiesing carefully reviewed the manuscript and in extensive comments answered all of my queries. Yet he also gave me all the liberty and confidence a translator could wish for. I am more than grateful for his enthusiastic involvement in the translation process.

-nfs-

ARTIFICIAL PRESENCE

Image Studies, Image Theory, and the Concept of the Image

Today, many have high hopes for a project variously called "image studies," "visual studies," or "visual culture" [*Bildwissenschaft*]. Yet, as is common with new academic disciplines, what specific tasks, contents, or methods should characterize image studies is controversial. Little can be deemed certain: a discipline that calls itself "image studies" dedicates itself to the study of the image. But a more detailed profile of the discipline requires further explanation. Is image studies an autonomous discipline on a par with other more traditional disciplines, such as archaeology and sociology? In that case there ought to be "image studies" majors in universities. Or is image studies perhaps part of an already known, established discipline, such as philosophy or art history? It could also be anchored in multiple disciplines, and in that case we could compare image studies to semiotics, which is used and studied in several fields as well. Yet it is just as conceivable that image studies belongs to one of those newer areas of study, like cultural or media studies, that are not yet fully determined as to scope and content. We cannot exclude the possibility that "image studies" does not denote any autonomous discipline at all but that it is merely a generic term that, on the basis of a kind of loose family resemblance, brings together various reflections on images, reflections that come from different disciplines and are heterogeneous in content and method. If this is the case, then it may be better not to speak about what image studies (in the singular) *is* but about what image studies (in the plural) *are*.

Facing such a lack of resolution, it is well worth returning to simple but secure basic distinctions. If we can assume that image studies investigates images, then we can safely say that in terms of pure extension, in terms of what the chosen topic comprises, we can distinguish three kinds of image studies: individual concrete images, a group of images, and the entirety of images can each be the topic of a study. Only these three kinds are conceivable. Thus, independent of any notion of content or method, the simple extension of the images selected, the choice of topic by itself gives rise to vastly divergent contributions to image studies.

The individual work as topic

In image studies the smallest conceivable thematic extension of a particular study is the single image. In this case we are dealing with theories about and descriptions of individual concrete objects, with explicit studies of single works. Thus, art historians may concern themselves with, for example, a special work of art, or psychologists of advertising with a concrete poster, each employing, with particular intentions, his or her specific disciplinary methods. Yet independent of the discipline in which a concrete image becomes the topic of a study, in all cases it is true that it becomes such only if the meaning of the image appears to justify this approach. And here the ambiguity of the concept of meaning is welcome, since "meaning" can be both the content or sense of something ("What does this street sign mean?") and the relevance of something ("My father means a lot to me"). In most instances an indissoluble mixture of both meanings of "meaning" functions as the occasion for concrete studies of images. As a result, every investigation of a single work is bound up with an appreciation. A special study inevitably turns an image into a special image, into one that is dealt with in a way that by no means every image is dealt with. For there to be a study of a concrete work, there must thus be a reason that lies in the work itself to justify this explicit thematization— and this, precisely, changes when we study groups of images.

The group of works as topic

Even a cursory glance at the steadily rising tide of publications on images shows that in most cases a more or less determinate group of images is thematized. The two extensional limit cases of work in image studies—individual concrete works and the phenomenon of pictoriality in principle—are more rarely to be found. This conclusion also holds regardless of the discipline from which specific reflections may arise. The lion's share of writing on images is dedicated to defined sets of concrete images. From the large number of conceivable criteria that can be used to form thematic subsets from the set of the entire stock of images, a canon has emerged of criteria that are commonly used to construct topics for image studies. We can discern the specific canonical rank of such a criterion by the fact that a study that employs a particular canonical criterion does not have to account for this employment. At the moment, art historians, for example, will hardly have to justify themselves to the community of art historians when they thematize certain images for the single reason that they form an artist's oeuvre. It is also perfectly "normal" for a historian of images to concentrate on that set of images that can be called "films." Others concentrate on images that are also at the same time woodcuts. The technique of production chosen and thematized in each case can be narrowed down even further. Such is the case when a study concentrates exclusively on digital films or mosaics, on frescoes or daguerreotypes. The place of production and the time of production are further ways of constituting topics that are as contingent as they are canonical. Yet what is truly remarkable is that in the same measure that determinate criteria have formed as canonical possibilities for *finding* a topic, possibilities for *combining* these criteria have established themselves in image studies as well. It is perfectly common, for example, to combine a technique of production with a place of production to define a downright typical object in image studies; exemplary for this is the mass of studies formed according to this schema: Roman mural paintings, American photography, French film, Greek mosaic. It is integral to the logic of this way of determining topics that this principle can be continued indefinitely, that even more, not just two, criteria can be and are combined. When Egyptian mummy portraits or the image of the president in the American press are studied, the author concentrates on a very limited group. This combination of contingent criteria provides a substantial part of studies in image studies with a topic. Typical studies have titles such as *Painting in Florence and Siena after the Great Plague*, *Gauguin and the Prints of the Pont-Aven School*, or *Scandinavian Paintings of Interiors in the Age of Carl Larson.* As distinct as the images thematized in these exemplary cases might be, the principle of definition is always the same. In all of these instances, the topic is the product of a contingent combination of criteria—and this is where, for image studies, a danger as well as, equally, an opportunity lies. The danger should be readily apparent. It consists in inadvertent emphasis and unwarranted pathos. This phenomenon is well known from literary studies, namely in the case of the problematic nature of editions of the collected works of great literary figures. Frequently such editions include, without any editorial distinction, the note a servant snatched from the paper bin against the will of the author, the unpublished triviality, or the ephemeral occasional poem on the same level as the poetical masterpiece. As a result, the incidental work receives a valorization, attention, and relevance that is not justified by the context in which it originally came about. This is no different when we look at groups of images.

Yet precisely this entry of what is artistically banal and inconsequential into the series of objects under investigation does not only harbor a danger but also a great opportunity: such an accommodation constitutes the first, necessary step toward a reflection on all images. No matter how idiosyncratic a group that is studied may be, as soon as a group and no longer a particularly relevant singular work is thematized, images unremarkable when taken by themselves are inevitably thematized by a field of study. This means that images become the object of a field of study for reasons that do not lie in their particular relevance. At the end of this development we find the philosophy of the image or, rather, we find what can and should be called "image theory." The turn toward the group is connected with an at least partial turn away from the masterpiece and the work of art. This process is especially important for the relation of art history to image studies. For as soon as the academic study of art concerns itself with groups of works, it can no longer concentrate exclusively on individual works of art. Since in art history images are thematized only because they are an element of a given group of images, art history—not just since Aby Warburg—has a built-in tendency toward a general image theory, that is, toward the idea to thematize images because they are part of the largest group possible, the group of all existing images. It is impossible to study images in art without being interested in all other images as possible comparative points of reference. To this extent there can be no doubt that there was—and still is—inherent in art history a disciplinary jurisdiction over all existing images. Yet this jurisdiction does not extend to the *concept* of the image. Art history, with its own methods, can and should concern itself with everything that is an image. But it cannot meaningfully be claimed that the engagement with the question *What is an image?* is an exercise in art history or art theory. For this question is a genuine category problem that cannot be answered historically or empirically. The question, rather, leads to yet another kind of theoretical interest in images. This is the interest in the concept of the image, which is a philosophical interest because defining the concept of the image is a problem that can only be solved philosophically. It is the task of *image theory*.

The concept of the image as topic

Enlarging the purview of the topic from a determinate group of works, no matter how large, to the concept of the image is not merely an extensional, quantitative enlargement but a step into the categorial. It necessarily demands a change of method. An image theory that attempts to talk about all objects that are images can, for reasons of principle, no longer be an empirical discipline—the reason is as simple as it is important: as soon as the task is to speak about all phenomena of pictoriality, the definition of which empirical objects belong to this category becomes highly problematic. A decidedly philosophical problem emerges. If we take the question *What is to be designated as an image?* seriously in all its radicality, asking it questions in general what objects are to be addressed as images. When we ask the question of the image in all its radicality, we can no longer presume that we know what objects are to be studied with respect to their common properties. Put differently, when we want to study all images theoretically, we primarily work on the question of what an image is and for what reasons something is an image—and this question, precisely, can only be answered with arguments. Every attempt at an empirical study of all images would perforce fail because of a problem that is specific to most philosophical problems. What is at stake is not an investigation of something already categorized but the investigation of categorization; what is at stake is the *concept* of the image. We are familiar with comparable problems from other philosophical disciplines. The morally good, for example, cannot be determined by studying actions "determined" to be morally good. In this case, too, we would have to know beforehand what actions can count as members of the group of morally good actions. Yet it is precisely this knowledge that is under discussion when we ask what is morally good. The parallel can easily be extended. In most cases hardly anyone would be confronted with the problem of not knowing which objects are images and which are not. Similarly, the moral evaluation of most actions is perfectly beyond dispute. Yet for the categorial investigation, this self-understood everyday knowledge cannot be assumed because it is to be thematized itself—especially since disputed, problematic cases are common not only in the domain of moral actions but in that of images as well.

It depends on one's specific philosophical position whether an astronomical constellation, mirror image, silhouette, calligram, diagram, abstract photography, cyberspace, a map, or footprint is counted among the group of images. In art theory the problem poses itself differently. Since not every work of art has to be an image, it is possible to think that monochrome painting created works of art but not images. Whether a monochrome painting can be an image is highly problematic, even if we are certain that it is, or can be, a work of art. Yet hardly anyone would want to enlarge the concept such that every monochrome surface would be an image. Therefore, if we want to address monochrome paintings as images, we have to explain why a canvas that is painted monochrome and has the status of art is an image while a monochrome surface that looks just the same but does not have the status of art should not be an image. This leads to the question of whether a specific context is decisive for the status of an object as image. Can the same object be an image in one place but not in another? Whatever one's position in relation to this problem is, no empirical finding will be able to help justify such a decision. Only the coherence of an argument about the sense of the concept of the image decides whether the objects in question are images. The number of problems becomes practically limitless when we ask whether the study of images implies studying those images that have no material existence at all, such as mental images, hallucinations, and visual imaginings. At the very least it is not uncommon, in philosophical and psychological studies, as well as in everyday speech, to speak of mental images. If such speech is justified, then the mental image must of course be a topic within the scope of image studies, that is, insofar as image studies really is ready to investigate all forms of pictoriality. The same problem poses itself in the study of linguistic images, for example tropic speech in metaphors. Works in literary and linguistic studies would become applied image studies (in the sense of working on a group of works) as soon as we are ready to accept metaphors as images, that is, as soon as we do not understand our speaking of "figurative speech" [*bildliche Rede*] to be metaphorical. In short, if we want to work theoretically on all images, if we want to know what forms of appearances are allowed for by the medium of pictoriality, we won't get anywhere if we do not reflect on the concept of the image. For we must decide which of the cases just outlined we want to include in our studies. Since this reflection on the concept of the image cannot take any other form than that of philosophy, we arrive at the conclusion that the philosophy of the image is part of the different forms of image studies or, conversely, that the different forms of image studies stand in need of a philosophy of the image. This philosophy of the image can simply be called image theory.

The Main Currents in Today's Philosophy of the Image

According to Aristotle, concepts can be determined by their *genus proximum* and a *differentia specifica*. Even though this traditional idea does not live up to the latest developments in modern theories of definition, it is exceptionally well suited to describe the dominant currents in today's philosophy of the image in an ideal typification. For it is not at all the case that for every object there must be only one *genus proximum*. For every object several genera can be found. Exactly what general phenomenon a concrete object belongs to is often a matter of dispute—and this seems to be confirmed today in the philosophy of the image and to lead to different currents within it. These competing currents are distinct, not least of all because they treat images as objects of different genera. We could also say that in today's philosophy of the image, opinions on the *genus proximum* diverge significantly. When, in an "Aristotelizing" manner, we set the main theses of established approaches next to one another, so to say, we can at least differentiate them in terms of an anthropological approach, a semiotic approach, and an approach based on perception [*wahrnehmungstheoretischer Ansatz*].[1]

For the *anthropological approach* images are, first of all, artifacts of the human; the genus "objects produced by human beings" is the *genus proximum*. Obviously, though, not all artifacts are always images. Among the many artifacts that exist, images are special things. To produce them, humans need specifically human skills, which is why image theory ought to be understood and practiced as a knowledge of the human. The *semiotic approach*, in contrast, places the concept of the image under a different genus: images are, first of all and necessarily, signs. Yet, once more, among the many existing signs, they form a special kind, which is why the specificity of the image within semiotics should constitute the genuine explorative interest of a philosophy of the image. In contrast, an *approach based on perception*—for example, the phenomenological approach—builds on the thought that all images are first of all visible objects. Here, too, the necessary characteristic of the image demands to be supplemented by a sufficient one. Among the many visible objects, images are distinguishable by having a distinctive form of visibility. This is why, from this perspective, the task of a philosophy of the image is to describe the kind of visibility that is characteristic of images.

The anthropological approach

Hans Jonas's classic essay "Homo pictor and the Differentia of Man" offers a paradigmatic impression of the specific concerns and strengths of the anthropological approach within the philosophy of the image. Jonas builds his argument on the thought that an image is an artifact humans alone are able to produce. If and when we find an image, we can suppose with certainty that it was produced by humans. Images might not be the only product with whose production we exclusively credit humans; yet that is not Jonas's argument. The special philosophical relevance of the human capacity to produce images becomes apparent only when the focus shifts away from concrete images toward the "conditions of image-making" in principle.[2] Exaggerating only slightly, we could say that Jonas does not turn to images because he is interested in images of any kind whatsoever, but because he wants to know "what properties are required in a subject for the making or beholding of images?"[3] Yet even this question does not reflect the real interest. The anthropological approach, according to Jonas, is not interested in those properties of the subject that make a production of images possible because they are the properties that make such productions possible. The reason, rather, is that these properties are identified with other properties. Jonas attributes an anthropological significance to the subjective preconditions that make productions of images possible—and in this respect, precisely, he remains prototypical for the anthropological approach up to this day: the conditions of possibility for the production of images are identical with the conditions of possibility of conscious, human existence. We are dealing with the following argumentative step: images are first examined so as to determine what transcendental preconditions are necessary for making use of the medium of the image. When these preconditions have been discerned in the images, nothing short of the anthropological preconditions for human being-in-the-world has been found.

Jonas sees the conditions of possibility for the production of images of any kind in the human capacity for the formation of ideas. Only a subject with ideas is able to generate depictions; the production of an image needs a capacity for mental pictoriality, the imagination. Undoubtedly—and Jonas does not fail to see this—this is only a necessary and by no means sufficient condition: "Images after all have to be made, not merely conceived. Thus their external existence as a result of human activity reveals also a physical aspect of the power that the image faculty wields: the kind of command that man has over his body."[4] We can only agree with Jonas here: some kind of skill or craft is necessary for the production of images as well: "only in this way can ideation [*Vor-stellung*] proceed to depiction [*Dar-stellung*]."[5] Yet what remains decisive is the precondition that must precede the skill and that forms the basis without which no skill could apply. For it is precisely this necessary precondition that can be interpreted as the fundamental capacity for abstraction and for the formation of ideas, as the capacity to form ideas of one's own perceivable situation of existence. As soon as a consciousness of world and existence forms, humans must step back from the world; that is, they must perceive the world as something that they, as the ones who perceive, are not: "Vision involved a stepping back from the importunity of environment and procured the freedom of detached survey. A stepping back of the second order takes place when appearance is comprehended *qua* appearance."[6] This very thesis of a stepping back of the second order is not specific to Hans Jonas's philosophy of the image. Rather, it runs like a guiding thread through image theories that argue anthropologically, that is, through theories that assign to images the role of displaying the conditions of human existence or even of consciousness. This basic assumption, at least, can be found in Vilém Flusser and Jean-Paul Sartre as well, in ways that are quite comparable to Jonas's argumentation.

Vilém Flusser, too, builds his image theory on the conviction that the most specifically human activity is not speaking but the capacity to produce images. We could even say that in this context Flusser speaks in terms astoundingly similar to Jonas's:

> Let us first look at the first image-making gesture. The image of a pony on the walls of the cave of Peche-Merle may serve as an example. When we try to reconstruct the gesture of such an early maker of images, we will for example say roughly the following: He stepped back from a pony, looked at it, then captured on the rock face what had been glimpsed fleetingly. . . . The fundamental question is, To where do we step back from the pony? We could think it sufficed to take a few steps back from the pony and enter a place somewhat more removed from it (for example onto a hill). We know from experience, however, that this description is not fully accurate. To make an image of the pony for ourselves, we have at the same time to somehow withdraw into ourselves. This strange nonplace [*Un-ort*] into which we thereby enter and from out of which we make images, in this tradition, has been signified by names such as "subjectivity" or "existence," for example like this: "Imagination" is the peculiar capacity to step back from the objective [*gegenständliche*] world into one's own subjectivity.[7]

Prior to Jonas and Flusser hardly anyone had more precisely elaborated this meaning of imagination (also called faculty of ideation or fantasy) than Jean-Paul Sartre in his classic study *L'Imaginaire* [*The Imaginary*]. From this perspective Sartre's phenomenological thought plays the role of a decisive precursor. For it is Sartre who asks the question "What must consciousness in general be?" in the context of a philosophy of the image: "We may therefore conclude that imagination is not an empirical power added to consciousness, but is the whole of consciousness as it realizes its freedom; every concrete and real situation of consciousness in the world is pregnant with the imaginary in so far as it is always presented as a surpassing of the real." Similar to Jonas and Flusser, Sartre works with a metaphor of distancing: "For consciousness to be able to imagine, it must be able to escape from the world by its very nature, it must be able to stand back from the world by its own efforts." To this "standing back" [*position de recul*] corresponds, in Jonas and Flusser, the stepping back, what Sartre describes as "to hold the real at a distance." Anyone who cannot step back from the world is, for Sartre, "glued down in the existent," like an object. Anyone who cannot perform this pictorial stepping back cannot be in the world in the mode of the human but can only "be 'in-the-midst of the world'": "If it were possible to conceive for a moment a consciousness that does not imagine, it would be necessary to conceive it as totally bogged down in the existent and without the possibility of grasping anything other than the existent." In short, "It is as absurd to conceive of a consciousness that does not imagine as it is to conceive of a consciousness that cannot effect the *cogito*."[8]

The examples of Jonas, Flusser, and Sartre, not in the same way yet to the same extent, stand for the central, fundamental thought in each and every anthropological image theory: the pictorial imagination is not just the condition of a specific human activity, namely the production of images; in the capacity for the production of images we are to see a condition of the possibility of consciousness and human existence. This key thought can also be put differently and systematically: to speak of internal and external images, of images in the mind and images on the wall, is not to equivocate. What is addressed equally in internal and external images is a consciousness of something that is not present. Anyone who watches a movie is, as viewer, conscious of a nonpresent reality, just like anyone who paints a situation in the imagination. For this reason the anthropological approach cannot look at images on the wall as separate from images in the mind—this, at least, is the consequence that Hans Belting elevates, making it the main thought of his *Bild-Anthropologie* [Anthropology of the Image]: "In the last analysis, the concept of the image, grasped at its root, is justified only as an anthropological concept. It cannot be separated from the twofold sense we endow it with when we speak of mental images just as we do of the artifacts of artistic and technical productions of images. In this way, the interaction of the imagination and technologies of the image is a quintessential anthropological topic."[9] With this, Belting explicates a further thesis specific to the anthropological approach. He shows, very convincingly, that the anthropological standpoint must programmatically turn against the distinction between "mental and physical images."[10] This "dualism" of two fundamental kinds of images is only an artificial construct. It cannot be maintained in the interaction with images because both forms of pictoriality "refer to one another in a variety of ways."[11] What Belting means is this: no beholding of an external image can do without the concourse of "memory and imagination."[12] Yet Belting goes even further: he advocates the idea that the proper "place of images" is by no means—as one might perhaps think—the museum, the wall, or the movie theater but "the human being" alone.[13] It is for no other reason that anthropology is to take up the baton from the discipline that up until now has concerned itself with images, that is, art history. The image is studied neither because it is a work of art nor because it is an image but because it helps answer questions that belong to an entirely different discipline, that is, to anthropology: "Anthropology thereby inherits the quest of the history of art, which the nineteenth century, sensing a loss of historical and artistic continuity, had invented."[14]

The anthropological approach within the philosophy of the image, whose most distinctive elaboration currently is Belting's, has not remained without its critics. To be sure, after Sartre no one wants to doubt the thesis of the mutual dependence of mental and material images. Who would seriously want to claim that in looking at and producing images, the imagination of the viewer and the image as physical object do not "refer to one another in a variety of ways"? Yet the question is what perspective emerges from this state of affairs for a general image theory. How can the anthropological relevance of the image be deployed in image theory? In particular, the soundness of Belting's conclusion that image theory can, for this reason, only be practiced as anthropology still needs a foundation. At the very least, as Tilman Reitz has objected in his essay "Der Mensch im Bild: Konservative Alternativen zur Kunstgeschichte" [The Human in the Image: Conservative Alternatives to Art History], the concern of the anthropological approach—a concern that is, in principle, understandable—almost has to develop an undifferentiated concept of the image. Such a concept must, for all the analogies it draws, skip over the differences:

The most critical situation, however, is that of the concept of the image itself. For one thing, the parallel of internal and external images only seems to be evident. This reveals itself for example in the erroneous assumption that in a motion picture the "mental images of the viewer" could "not unambiguously be distinguished from the images of the technical fiction." In fact, it is precisely this simple distinction between a visible artifact to which we can return by indicating or explaining it and mental events accessible only to the perceiver as visual occurrence [*Geschehen*] that makes it difficult theoretically to study "internal images" in the first place.[15]

Indeed, here as elsewhere the impression arises that the anthropological approach is to a worrisome degree sustained by treating equivocations and analogies as identities. This procedure is apparent in at least two places that are quite central to the argumentation of the anthropology of the image.

First, we have the fundamental anthropological idea that images are essentially human images [*Bilder vom Menschen*]. Yet this very formulation can clarify what ambiguity is at play here. Images are produced by humans, and often they can also be about humans; that is, they can picture humans. These are the two different meanings of "human images." A lack of distinction between these two relations of the image to the human leads the anthropological consideration of the human-made image to concentrate—without reason and in not just a few cases—on images that, among other things, display humans or have specifically human themes. This leads in turn to an implicit valorization of images with specific content, as if the images that display humans were *the* anthropologically authentic and true images, as if it were possible to assume that every image was "brought about by supratemporal themes such as death, body, and time."[16] Moreover, this is a constriction to specific images and, interestingly, to those images for which it might still be possible to find art historical arguments, even though it is precisely art history that is to be anthropologically superseded. Art historically, we might still want to say that in the West those images that display humans possess a special relevance. In no case, however, can the images that show humans and bodies be said to be of greater relevance for a media philosophy of the image than are images with a different content. Tilman Reitz is thus perfectly justified when he remarks that all the enthusiasm for the anthropological approach prevents a discussion of its basic assumptions and that "later, the question of why it is that general image theory only ever speaks of the depiction of human bodies hardly ever comes up."[17]

Second, the danger that anthropological thinking turns into metaphorical anthropomorphism becomes even clearer when we speak of death in images. We find this not just in Belting; it is a favorite beyond the anthropological approach as well: "The photographed human, when his movement was frozen in the photograph, resembled a living dead person. The new image that so emphatically demonstrated life in truth produced a shadow."[18] As a matter of fact, it is beyond dispute that many viewers think they can see in an image something that is not in attendance. In this respect there is of course the possibility that it is specific to the medium of the image "that inescapably something withdraws from us."[19] Furthermore, we can say that humans, when they die, inescapably withdraw from those they leave behind. Yet when what is pictorially displayed, as a whole, is for this reason addressed as a dead something, we are dealing with an identification of analogies. We could also call this a metaphorical way of speaking that is understandable provided we know that the argument works with the idea that true images always display humans anyway. Yet understandable as the genesis of this methaphorics may be, it cannot for that reason claim validity.

The semiotic approach

Any form of mystification that turns the image into the authentic place of an absolute truth, of death, or of authentic existence is foreign to the semiotic approach within the philosophy of the image. Its rather formal and sober mode of argumentation is nowhere better encountered than in Nelson Goodman's *Languages of Art*. With appreciable clarity it projects and develops the key thought of a decidedly semiotic image theory—including the thesis, typical of this approach, that the medium of the image does not stand in need of an independent philosophy of the image. The problems of such a philosophy, from this standpoint, are not of so special a kind as to warrant the foundation of a philosophical subdiscipline. A fully elaborated philosophy of language is sufficient. With such a philosophy of language, according to Goodman, we can answer the questions of general image theory. It is for this very reason that Goodman refers to his *Languages of Art* not as an image theory but as a "general theory of symbols."[20]

The argument that general image theory is a subdiscipline of a general theory of symbols builds on the supposition that images necessarily are signs. Or, put differently, an object that is not a sign cannot be an image.

The particularity of the image, accordingly, is exclusively intrasemiotic—a thought that can already be found in all desirable perspicuity in the writings of Charles Sanders Peirce, the father of modern semiotics. For Peirce, "icon" is a concept on a par with the concepts "index" and "symbol"; together these describe the three conceivable kinds of signs. In a semiotic philosophy of the image, images exist exclusively as a particular form of the sign. This does not mean, however, that within this current, opinions cannot diverge. Particularly in reference to the question of what the intrasemiotic particularity of the image consists in, there is no consensus. Peirce argues that an icon can be distinguished from symbols and indexes by the resemblance of the icon and the signified object [*Bezeichnetes*]. In contrast, Goodman, who uses the concepts "symbol" and "sign" synonymously, emphasizes that images precisely cannot be distinguished from other forms of symbolizing by means of resemblance: "The plain fact is that an image, to represent an object, must be a symbol for it, stand for it, refer to it; and that no degree of resemblance is sufficient to establish the requisite relationship of reference. Nor is resemblance *necessary* for reference; almost anything may stand for almost anything else. An image that represents—like a passage that describes it—an object refers to and, more particularly, *denotes* it. Denotation is the core of representation and is independent of resemblance."[21] If we take this thought seriously, it leads us to think that images are images of the things they are images of by reason of conventions that are learned and not by reason of visible resemblance.[22]

Semiotic philosophies of the image might differ in respect to the question of the image's resemblance, yet the view that images are signs in the first place is wholly uncontested. The basis of the semiotic approach is the transformation of a distinction taken from image theory into the language of semiotics. What is meant here is a classic distinction that can be found in nearly every philosophy of the image, a distinction Hans Jonas has succinctly formulated: "the represented, the representation, and the vehicle of representation (the imaging thing, or physical carrier of the image) are different strata in the ontological constitution of the image."[23] Whether it is necessary to understand this structure ontologically, as Jonas does, is a negligible question. What is decisive is that in precise speech about images we must differentiate between the depicted, the depiction, and the depicting, and that the different approaches within the philosophy of the image agree in this regard; only in further interpreting this tripartition do different points of view emerge. It therefore makes sense to take a closer look at the semiotic interpretation of this tripartition.

When we have an image hanging on the wall, we can determine in it a depicting image carrier, which consists, for example, of paper or of canvas and oil paint. An image's depicting material can be described physically. Yet an image does not only consist of those aspects that can be determined and described physically. An object is an image only when it is not just a flat object on a wall but also a depiction. The depiction aspect of the image can be clearly distinguished from the depicting material since the depiction—in Jonas's felicitous phrase—is "removed from the causal commerce of things."[24] This is precisely not the case for a mirror: in a mirror we can see only things that are subject to the laws of physics. What we see in the mirror, optically mediated, are actually present things but not images of things. An image, which in respect to its materiality might consist of paper, in a different respect is a depiction, for example the depiction of a house. When we are dealing with an image of a house, this exclusively visible house is removed from the laws of physics. The depiction of the house does not age insofar as the house displayed does not age, even if the image carrier does of course age, like any other physical object in space and time. Anyone who looks at an image from the side nonetheless does not look at the depiction from the side; even though light falls onto an image, the object displayed in the image is not lit up. These criteria for the determination of a depiction are as simple as they are decisive. Besides the depicting image carrier and the depiction given in the image, we must also take note of the third aspect of the image, of the depicted. By the depicted we mean the real object to which some viewer of an image refers by means of the image.

From the semiotic point of view, the interpretation of this tripartition is unambiguous: the tripartition *depicting-depiction-depicted* corresponds to the three familiar aspects of each and every sign. We know the tripartition under different names. In semiotics the depicting image carrier is variously called sign carrier (or sign vehicle), token, or signifier; what is meant is always the same: the means of signifying. The visible depiction in the image corresponds to what, for the sign, is called its content, sense designated, or its intension. In all these cases what is meant are the properties that are determined by a sign or, as the case may be, by an image. Thanks to these properties named by the sign, there is the possibility to refer to a concrete object in the physical world. As we know, we can refer to one and the same object both by means of naming and by means of depicting different properties. This object, also called reference object, meaning, or extension, does not have to be really existent. The phenomenon that there are depictions of fictional things is familiar from many signs, signs that make sense but do not have any meaning.

In short, the semiotic approach sees in the tripartition *depicting-depiction-depicted* nothing but the mode of appearance proper to images of the differentiation of *sign carrier–intension–extension*. The analogy of these two tripartitions suggests this idea—yet what suggests itself is not necessarily correct. Once more we must be careful not to hastily turn an analogy into a false identity. An object indeed becomes a sign only when it is assigned a content, a sense, or a meaning. In this regard we can only agree with Klaus Sachs-Hombach: "An object is a sign already thanks to our assigning it a content or a meaning."[25] Yet this is not the solution but precisely the problem. Must we assign a content or a meaning to an image? Must we interpret the depiction as content? Is what the image depicts the content of a sign simply thanks to the image's depicting it? Have we assigned a sense to a surface merely by seeing a depiction on this surface? If that were the case, then all images would always be signs.

The approach based on perception

We can gain a particularly clear impression of the perception-based counterposition to the analytical approach from Konrad Fiedler's and Edmund Husserl's philosophies of the image. Their two key concepts are nonsemiotic attempts to answer the question, *What are the depiction, the depicting, and the depicted?*[26] As is to be expected, the particularity of their answer is not found in an explanation of the depicting and the depicted. In this regard the only differences among the several approaches within image theory are terminological. The terminology coined by Husserl calls the depicting material "image carrier" [*Bildträger*] and the real object to which an image can refer "image subject" [*Bildsujet*]. What is decisive is the name he suggests for the depiction that visibly appears in the image: from 1901 on, Husserl speaks of the "image object" [*Bildobjekt*][27]—and this is a decidedly antisemiotic counterconcept.

Husserl interprets the depiction in the image not as a form of sense or content but as a kind of object, an image object. He does so because he wants to give depiction in an image a special ontological status: he describes the depiction as a special object that becomes visible in an image—which is not to say that what appears is a real object. Not everything that has the properties of a real physical object must itself be a real physical object. The image object is not a real object; it is exclusively the object that is described when someone says what he or she thinks he or she sees on an image carrier. The image object is the motif [*Motiv*] of an image. The image object, therefore, is always an object for someone. We could say it is a phenomenon in the image. As long as nobody looks at the image carrier, there will be no image objects. The image object is what is meant by the viewer of the image; that is, it is an intentional object. The reason for this interpretation of depiction as a supposed object is as simple as it is convincing: we can see the image object. That, at least, is how it appears to us viewers of images: it appears as the object of a perception. In contrast, we cannot see a sense or a content. For the sense of a sign is a rule about how we can refer to something by means of that sign. Rules, however, cannot be perceivable. That is why for Husserl a depiction is not a form of symbolized sense but a form of artificial presence.

The idea of an artificial presence produced by images is like a thread running through phenomenological image theory and can be regarded as its main idea. Jean-Paul Sartre puts this perspective in particularly clear and succinct terms in his essay "What Is Literature?": "The painter does not want to paint signs onto the canvas, he wants to create a thing. . . . He is therefore as far as he can be from considering colours and signs as a *language*. . . . But, you will say, suppose the painter portrays houses? That's just it. He *makes* them, that is, he creates an imaginary house on the canvas and not a sign of a house."[28] The idea is unambiguous: anyone who produces an image does not create a sign but a particular kind of object: an image object, an imaginary house—or, as Fiedler would say, a "visibility construct" [*Sichtbarkeitsgebilde*].[29] He creates a merely visible house, an object of pure visibility. For none of the positions in perception theory would be of the absurd opinion that there is no difference between the presentation of a real thing (for example in a shop window or on a tray) and the artificial presence of an image object. An object with real presence in the world is necessarily an object that behaves according to the laws of physics, which in turn means that it can act physically on the human body; to speak of real presence is not a pleonasm. The concept of real presence specifies presence [*Präsenz*] in terms of a worldly kind of presentness [*Gegenwärtigkeit*] with substantial attendance [*Anwesenheit*]. That is why there can be a nonreal, an artificial, presence—a presence, precisely, without substantial attendance. Images are not windows, yet their particular way of displaying can still be described by comparisons with other ways of displaying. In opposition to shop windows, images present things that are not real things. Things in images are exclusively visible and never collect dust. Fiedler's speaking of pure visibility is a description of the particular kind of being-an-object—he speaks explicitly of a "form of being"[30]—that distinguishes the image object: it is necessarily an object that is exclusively visible and must therefore be an "immaterial construct" [*stoffloses Gebilde*][31] without physics. The concept "pure" in this context means that the image is "exclusively" and "only" visible. As in Kant, "pure" is the opposite of "attached." The visibility of a pictorially depicted thing is not attached to a substance that could also be perceived by other senses. The implication of presence and substantiality dissolves in the image. What we see in the image has no material substance. For this reason the production of an image, for Sartre, is a process that can be described as "disembodied";[32] Fiedler calls the same process one of "isolating," of "dissociating" and "separating."[33] Pure visibility originates in the isolation of an attached visibility, and it is in just this way that the disembodied visibility of something not in attendance is constructed. We could also say with Fritz Heider that image objects are "false unities."[34] For in the image something is seen as a unity that is not materially or causally conditioned. When we see a human depicted in an image, we see the body as a unity even though the depicted head is not physiologically connected to the depicted foot, which is simply the case for real unities (for real human beings). The communality is clear: images, in this tradition of perception theory, are understood as a medium with which it becomes possible to produce a nonphysical yet still visible object sui generis (even though this object is addressed differently, as image object, imaginary thing, pure visibility, or false unity).

The difference between the semiotic approach and the approach based on perception

The difference between the semiotic approach and the approach based on perception arises from the distinct interpretations they give of the uncontested differentiation of the depicting, the depiction, and the depicted. The semiotic approach interprets this tripartition in this way:

1. depicting = sign vehicle or sign carrier;
2. depiction = sense or content;
3. depicted = meaning or reference object.

The approach based on perception interprets the tripartition in this way:

1. depicting = image carrier;
2. depiction = image object or imaginary object or pure visibility;
3. depicted = image subject.

We can see in this juxtaposition the essential difference between the two approaches: it is not the question of the image's resemblance that separates them. What is important is the mutual reproach that the other approach commits a fundamental category mistake. They reproach each other for identifying depiction with something that it is not. Since identification of the nonidentical constitutes a metaphor, we can say that they reproach each other for being entangled in metaphors: "When Sartre, for example, speaks of imaginary houses that the painter creates, he seems to me to metaphorically indicate nothing but the content or the meaning of the image."[35] A phenomenologist, in contrast, would say that the identification of the depiction that appears with a symbolized content is an identification of the nonequivalent and therefore a metaphorical act that identifies the triadic structure of the sign with the triadic structure of the image. This metaphorical speech of the content of an image becomes particularly clear when we turn to the form of the image's reception.

The interpretation of depiction as image object, as well as the interpretation of depiction as content, is linked to determinations concerning how the depiction is received. For Goodman the way we receive an image is in any case a reading: "Images in perspective, like any others, have to be read; and the ability to read has to be acquired."[36] If the image has a sense and refers to something, it is indeed appropriate to describe the reception of the image as a reading. If, however, the image presents an image object, then it is inapt to suppose that images are read, for image objects are not read but seen. Shop windows are not read but looked at. The result is that in the approach based on perception images are seen—the recipient of the image is a viewer—while for the semiotic approach they are read. The two kinds of dealing with images are categorially different. In the case of reading we are dealing with a following of rules; in the case of seeing we are dealing with a sensual consciousness of the presentness of something. Yet when an image is seen, this something is by no means a real object but precisely an imaginary object, a false unity that is present as such [*als eine solche präsent ist*]. The viewer of an image sees that he or she sees an image of something and not the thing itself. This clarifies the decisive point of the argument. What is important is not the second but the first part of Goodman's already quoted view: "The plain fact is that an image, to represent an object, must be a symbol for it, stand for it, refer to it; and that no degree of resemblance is sufficient to establish the requisite relationship of reference."[37] The claim that no degree of resemblance is sufficient to establish the requisite relationship of reference is so ubiquitous that we are likely to find it in practically every image theory; Husserl, at least, explicitly writes as early as 1901: "Resemblance between two objects, however great it may be, does not make the one an image of the other."[38] It has to be clearly said: it has probably never been claimed by anyone that resemblance is sufficient for pictoriality. Goodman's criticism is convincing, yet it remains the criticism of a fictional position. The really relevant question, rather, is whether an image must always be a representation and thus always be a reference. No one denies that two things do not have to stand in a relation of reference to one another merely because they possess a resemblance perceivable by a viewer. From this Goodman concludes that resemblance cannot be important for images. Yet he can only draw this conclusion because he furthermore assumes that images have a reference object. With this second premise his conclusion is indeed correct. Yet the second premise that images always refer to something is not convincing at all. Instead it expresses the implicit assumption that the objects of the humanities always refer to something, which means, in the end, that they always have a sense that must be brought to the light of day by an interpretation. What distinguishes the approach based on perception is the idea that we can give up on the idea that images *necessarily* refer. It stands for a certain fundamental orientation of work in the humanities. Images, accordingly, possess visible properties that cannot be transformed into sense, meaning, or text, and they thus withdraw from any discipline whose sole effort is to explore symbolized sense. As Hans Ulrich Gumbrecht describes in *Production of Presence: What Meaning Cannot Convey*, when an opinion settles on "how tired we are in the humanities of a repertoire of analytic concepts that can only give us access to the dimension of meaning,"[39] what manifests itself is not just a phenomenological interest in the artificial presence of image objects but a turn to phenomena of presence in general. Seen this way, the approach within image theory that is based on perception, too, mirrors a discontent with "an *institutional* configuration within which the absolute dominance of meaning-related questions had long led to the abandonment of all other types of phenomena and questions."[40]

It is easily understandable that the exploration of phenomena of presence seems to have particularly thrived in image theory. To display something pictorially precisely does not mean that something is referred to by means of the image. It means that something is artificially presented: it is made visible—and for the moment that's it. There is the possibility that with the image something that is visible and resembles something else is produced. But as Goodman himself says, what resembles does not have to refer. Images can display and present something. In images, too, viewers can become familiar with properties of the image object by looking at it. They can count the windows of Sartre's imaginary house on the side that is displayed. But looking at and studying a thing—even an image object—does not turn this thing into a sign, does not give meaning to it. Signs arise from use, not from looking at something. That is why images, like all other things, can be signs as well; but they do not have to be. It is against this backdrop in particular that it is well worth trying to describe the case—certainly not uncommon—of images being used as signs.

When Images Are Signs:
The Image Object as Signifier

When we engage the question of whether images are signs, we must consider the following distinction: on the one hand, there are questions that are answered by determining properties; on the other hand, there are questions that are answered by indicating functions. An exemplary question for the first case would be *Are dolphins fish?* This question is answered exclusively by establishing specific empirical properties: dolphins must be examined biologically to determine whether they have the properties of fish or not. Since it is well known that they do not have these properties, we know that they are not fish. This is different in the case of the second type, as the question *Are flowers gifts?* can show. This question is not answered by naming the properties of flowers; that would be entirely inapt. An object becomes a gift exclusively by serving a certain function. Therefore, in order to know whether these concrete flowers are a gift, we have to find out what is being done with them.

The question *Are images signs?* is of this second type; it is concerned with functions. This is not because of the images but is exclusively due to the fact that the concept of the sign is a functional concept. This does not change when the sign character of images is taken into account. Signs are like gifts: neither exists in a physical sense; no lab, however advanced it may be, can with its methods find out which flowers are a gift or what object is a sign. Max Bense felicitously opens his *Semiotik* [Semiotics] with this appraisal of the unavoidable functional character of signs: "Everything is a sign that is declared to be a sign, and only that which is declared to be a sign."[1] This is why, elsewhere, he rightly encourages us to make sure "that a sign not simply be introduced as a special object, but as a 'function,' as a something that 'functions.'"[2] He concludes from this that "in principle every arbitrary something can serve as a sign if only it is conceived of as such, interpreted as such."[3] Charles Sanders Peirce, too, admits of no doubt in the matter of this functional character of signs: "nothing is a sign unless it is interpreted as a sign."[4] With the later Wittgenstein we could also say, more emphatically: "Every sign *by itself* seems dead. *What* gives it life?—In use it is *alive*."[5]

To identify a certain object as a sign, the functional character of signs compels us to describe a specific mode of usage. We must describe what is being done with a thing. This can be done rather simply. Fortunately, there is not much controversy about what specific purpose signs fulfill. Peirce, for example, describes the specific function of the sign in this way: "A sign is an object which stands for another to some mind."[6] According to this view an object becomes a sign precisely when someone uses it to refer to something. All things that serve the function of making reference to something are signs. Since it has become common in recent years to use the concept of the symbol as a mere synonym of the concept of the sign, we can also say that signs are precisely those objects that are used for symbolizing. From the point of view of these objects, the characteristic of being a sign is something that happens to them: without their having anything to do with it, some things become signs—and the same happens to some images.

There is no reason to assume that pictorial signs constitute an exception to the general functional character of all signs. Since we cannot tell whether a sign is a sign merely by looking at it, we cannot, when we look at an image, tell whether it is a sign. If that were the case, images would be the first objects to have meaning on their own. Yet as long as we are not willing to accept such a sign character [*Zeichenhaftigkeit*] that would be given in itself, we must assume that some kind of usage turns images, too, into signs. This means that every image *can* be a sign, and no image *has to* be a sign—and it is for this very reason that the question *Are images signs?* is not particularly well put. A better formulation brings the systematic problem touched on here into focus: when are images signs? Or, asked differently: what has to be done for an image to become a sign? By themselves, these more precise formulations clarify that the thesis *There are certain images of which we know that they are not signs*, as well as the opposite thesis, *Every image is always a sign*, equally ignore that the sign character [*Zeichencharakter*] of things is, in any case, the result of a function. Against this background it is extremely peculiar that we can still discern, in today's philosophy of the image, a fierce discussion of these two theses, just as if the principle *tertium non datur* applied in this context. In the end we can only be surprised to observe that the pseudo-alternative of these two opinions has become a staple of discussions in image theory.

The current discussion of the question of the sign in the philosophy of the image

Phenomenologists, like image theorists and philosophers who determine the image from the perspective of perception theory generally, advocate a conception that Reinhard Brandt puts concisely: "Images can but they do not have to function as signs."[7] This constitutes a decidedly functionalist understanding of the sign. The only problem is that even this unambiguously functionalist view can be obscured by an unfortunate rendering, such that a completely different opinion arises—and this happens rather often. Indeed it is easy to find examples, such as Winfried Nöth's case, where the phenomenological position is understood and rendered as if the claim were made that "images were not always signs."[8] This means that the view *Images can but they do not have to function as signs* is identified with the opinion *Images are not always signs*. Yet this translation and identification are unfortunate, for they switch from a functionalist language ("images function") to a substantialist language ("images are") and thereby facilitate a grave misunderstanding. For the proposition *Images are not always signs* sounds like a proposition that can only be understood extensionally—for example: *Cars are not always sedans*. The translation thus suggests that in the discussion of the sign character of images we can find an advocacy of a "thesis of the non-sign character [*Nichtzeichenhaftigkeit*] of some images"[9] in the sense that in the set of all images, some images would not possess the properties of signs. Yet precisely this substantialist interpretation of the sign is to be avoided by the precise formulation *Images can but they do not have to function as signs*. It is the extensional interpretation of the idea that not all images are signs that leads to the opposite thesis, that of the "sign character of all images," being demonstrated by an explicit engagement with "images without reference objects."[10] In these cases—those of fictional and abstract images—the problematic sign character of these types of images is specially to be shown. Yet it is by means of this procedure that a suggestion made at the beginning of this chapter turns into an explicit supposition, namely that the position that is criticized had indeed claimed that there were certain types of images that would not be signs—in principle. It is only through this criticism that an opinion arises that nobody in the study of contemporary image theory advocates and that we would be hard-pressed to find an advocate for in the history of philosophy: the opinion that in the case of certain images it were possible to show by means of the images themselves that they are not signs.

The opposite view, however, that all images in themselves always have to be signs, is defended quite often. Roland Posner and Dagmar Schmauks, for example, write that "images are a particular partial region of the visible, namely surface artifacts [*flächenhafte Artefakte*], that are at the same time signs in that they picture [*abbilden*] something."[11] Winfried Nöth, too, explicitly defends "the premise of the sign character of all images."[12] We can say that this view forms the programmatic basis of image semiotics, which perceives the sense of its activity to depend on the observation that all images are always signs. We do not have to see it this way; we could very well imagine image semiotics as a sensible and necessary discipline for the study of those images that are used as signs. Yet this limitation to the semiotically employed image would render the semiotic claim to universality invalid; in that case image theory could no longer be understood as a mere subdiscipline of semiotics. This is where the proper interest of semiotics in the essential sign character of all images comes from. This interest is described candidly: "To speak of semiotic foundations of image theory means to start from the premise that images are signs, for if semiotics wants to contribute anything fundamental to image theory, the premise of the sign character of images must be valid."[13] Correspondingly, Klaus Sachs-Hombach writes in the foundational work of a general image theory, his *Das Bild als kommunikatives Medium* [The Image as Communicative Medium]: "Semiotic image theories suppose a close connection between the concept of the image and the concept of the sign. Images, accordingly, are signs."[14]

What refers when images refer to something?

If we want to distance ourselves from the discussion of this ostensible alternative—*Images are always signs* vs. *There are images that are not signs*—a question that sounds surprising at first becomes relevant: What is it that refers to something when someone refers to something with an image? It should be beyond dispute that the function of the sign is a function of relation. In the case of the image, however, the terms of this relation are in no way self-evident. Put differently: What is it that in an image takes on the function of serving as a sign? What is it that someone uses when someone uses an image as a sign? These questions sound idiosyncratic and do not belong to the canonical problems of contemporary image semiotics. The reason is fairly obvious: it seems as if the answer were already contained in the question. What refers when images refer to something is these very images. As true as this may be, it is unclear just what is meant by the word *image*. This lack of clarity is more easily perceived when we compare images to nonpictorial signs, since for the latter the question of what is used to refer can be clearly answered.

Think of a stop sign. In this case we can easily say what is referred to what: a physically describable object—namely, the red and white stop sign—is used as a sign for the order to stop one's car at this point. It is accepted common usage to label as "signifier" the object that is used as a sign for something.[15] Furthermore, there should be no doubt that in most cases signs have a material signifier. In the case of the written word we have a signifier that is made of ink. Depending on the semiotic theory and tradition, several concepts for the signifier have currency: *sign carrier* (or *sign vehicle*), *sign occurrence, means of signifying, the referring,* or even *the designating.* The *termini technici* "expression" or "token" are widespread as well. The discussion of the problems at hand is made even more difficult by these different terminologies. For no fewer concepts have gained acceptance to name that to which a sign refers, what is meant and signified. In the semiotics of the image we could use the concepts *meaning, denotatum, referent, signified*, and *designated* as synonymous for what is meant by the pictorial sign. In short, the signifier is that object that, by being used as a sign, becomes a sign for a signified. In the cases of stop signs, words, emblems, gestures, we are dealing with a material signifier—and this is precisely not the case for images, which brings us to the decisive semiotic particularity of pictorial signs.

Whenever images are used as signs, an immaterial signifier is used as a sign. This is so even when material images are at issue, be they photographs, films, paintings, mosaics, posters, woodcuts, or drawings. Peculiar as this idea may seem at first, it is what emerges when the question just raised is answered, a question that for this reason, and despite its idiosyncrasy, is extraordinarily relevant to image theory. What does the word *image* mean in the sentence *The image refers* [bezieht sich] *to something*? This question assumes that what functions as a signifier when an image functions as a sign is not understood as a matter of course. Imagine somebody looks at a photograph and says, "The image refers [*verweist*] to New York." Such propositions can be found in all currents of contemporary image theory. The central theme of Nelson Goodman's *Languages of Art* is "the relation between an image and what it represents."[16] But what does *image* mean here? This theme and this formulation are anything but an isolated case. There is probably no book about images that remains silent about the symbolic relations of images. Sentences such as *The image is a symbol for this and that* or *The photograph stands for this and that* can be found easily and often in everyday life and in image theoretical contexts; not to speak of propositions as subtle as *Images always refer to images* or *The image refers to itself.* As widespread as speaking of symbolic images and of reference with images might be, the problem remains the same: it is not at all clear what is meant by the concept "image." Since *image* has at least three distinct possible meanings, there is a downright equivocation of several concepts of the image. That is why it is peculiar that, even though on the one hand images are constantly claimed to refer to something, to mean something, and to symbolize something, there is, on the other hand, no pertinent discussion of the question of what the concept "image" really means in those propositions. Yet if only for the sake of correctly understanding, in each case, the claims about symbolic references with images, never mind for the sake of evaluating their truth content, it must be clear what, in each case, is meant by *image*. The entity that refers when an image refers is obscured by an equivocation—an equivocation that, like most equivocations, mostly does not cause any difficulties of understanding in everyday life but, even so, must be differentiated for precise semiotic consideration.

Three meanings of image

In sentences such as *There is an image on the wall, The image is torn, Put more light on the image,* or *That must have been an expensive image,* we understand the word *image* just as well as we understand the phrase "put some money on" in the sentence *I put some money on that horse. Image* in these instances signifies what should more precisely be called "image carrier" or "physical image." With *image* we address a material entity, for we can only touch, put on the wall, or shine light on a physical object; it is a certain real thing that is bought for a large sum of money. Yet this first meaning of *image*, in the sense of image carrier, is not the only meaning the word *image* can have.

A second meaning can be found in sentences such as *Rarely have I seen images as boring.* In this sentence the same word, *image,* is used; it sounds the same and is spelled the same way, but it has a different meaning from that in the sentence *The image is torn.* In a proposition about boring images what is meant is no longer the image carrier but exclusively the visible depiction. The same is true for the sentences *The images have a great spatial depth* or *In the image Peter is standing in front of the car.* When a motion picture is rated "R," what is meant by the interdiction is exclusively that which becomes visible and not the visible roll of film—any child could look at the roll of film. This concerns the classical distinction between image object and image carrier. For indeed the word *image* is used for both the image carrier and for that which we should better call, with Husserl, the "image object." The image object is that object that becomes visible on an image carrier. In the Göttingen lecture "Phantasie und Bildbewußtsein" ["Phantasy and Image Consciousness"], given in the winter semester 1904–5 and definitive in this context, Husserl describes the image object as "something appearing that has never existed and never will exist and, of course, is not taken by us for even a moment as something real."[17] We may very well say that a canvas becomes an image carrier only by virtue of an image object's becoming visible on it to someone as a phenomenon. Even though there is neither an image object without an image carrier nor an image carrier without an image object, we can easily distinguish these related phenomena, both conceptually and empirically, because they look so different. This we can easily observe if we ask someone to describe the way the canvas looks or the way the depiction looks. This is why, despite their equioriginality [*Gleichursprünglichkeit*], image carrier and image object are not the same thing. For the image viewer at the moment of viewing the image carrier, the image object is an intentional object—as Husserl writes: a "nonthing supposedly appearing to us as present"[18]—in opposition to the image carrier, which is supposedly a real thing. Or, put more precisely, the image carrier appears to the viewer as a real thing of which he or she believes that it is really present.

The result of these reflections is the following: the distinction between image carrier and image object shows that we are dealing with "a serious equivocation."[19] The image object (the depiction that becomes visible) and the image carrier (the material that makes the depiction visible) are often addressed in short—which is not problematic—in everyday life, but equally—which is annoying—in image theoretical contexts as "image." Precisely for the sake of precision and simple intelligibility we would best completely refrain from using the word *image* and always say precisely what we mean in a given instance. We could also somewhat paradoxically take this a step further: image theory will make progress if it speaks less of images—especially since there is yet a third meaning.

The third meaning of the word *image* can be found in sentences such as *Though the image is more than a hundred years old, its political message remains highly relevant* or *I have yet to take a closer look at the images in the exhibition*. In these sentences the word *image* stands for that which encompasses both the image carrier and the image object. Particularly tricky, philosophically, is for example the rather banal sentence, *The image is hung upside down*. Only an image carrier can hang on a wall, but only an image object can be upside down. In this sentence we thus address the unity of both. It is perfectly normal to speak of the *image carrier of an image* or of the *image object of an image*. That is only possible, however, when *image* can mean not only either image carrier or image object. Image carrier and image object are the two aspects of an image (here in the sense of unity). They are the two aspects of the image that we can look at, if not in the same way at least to the same extent.

In short, at least three distinguishable phenomena are frequently addressed in certain contexts by the word *image*, and each time this address is an abbreviation: the image carrier, the image object, and the unity of both. This equivocation would do no further harm if it were always clear what in each case was meant by *image*. But this, precisely, is not the case at all. This is where the propositions that describe a symbolic reference of images enter into play once more. In their case it is hardly clear in a readily intelligible way what meaning of the concept of the image is used. The claim *The image denotes Peter* is as intelligible as the sentence *The ball is beautiful*. Just as we do not know whether it is the football or the inaugural ball that is beautiful, we cannot understand whether it is the image object, the image carrier, or the unity of both that refers to Peter. The semiotically decisive question is therefore this: Does the concept "image" in the proposition *The image denotes Peter* mean the same as the concept "image" in the proposition *The image is destroyed* or as in the proposition *The image is exciting*?

The same problem of intelligibility repeats itself in the discussion of the resemblance of images. In strict parallel we find propositions everywhere that affirm or deny that images bear resemblance to what they denote. It is, for example, a widespread (but also criticized) view that there is a relation of resemblance between the image and the thing pictured. Yet before we discuss this view, it must be clear what the terms of this relation of resemblance are supposed to be. Is what is meant by the object designated as "image" (which is supposed to bear resemblance to something else) the image object or the image carrier? This means that the problem consists in answering the question *What bears resemblance to something when it is affirmed or denied that an image bears resemblance to something else?* Thus, for example, Klaus Rehkämper rightly stresses that the "theory of resemblance enters the debate when the question is how such an object—the image—produces a relation of representation to its signified [*Denotat*]."[20] Yet what we call "image" is precisely not such *an* object, for *two* objects are called "image." What meaning does the concept "image" have in these propositions? For the discussion of resemblance, too, we can only repeat what we have already said: we have to speak less of the image when we speak about images.

The image object, an immaterial signifier

At first sight it seems obvious that every time anyone observes that an image refers to something, what is meant by *image* is the image carrier. This view imposes itself for reasons of analogy: as with other signs, what we have in the case of the image is a material sign that can be printed onto a page just like material letters. Indeed, all nonpictorial signs have accustomed us to the image carrier's being a material occurrence. This is why it is practically self-understood for semiotics of different traditions to assume that in the case of pictorial signs, too, the signifier must be a physical occurrence; Roland Barthes' studies, for example, typify this prejudice. In his case this view does not have to be extracted from his writings; he explicitly articulates it: "therefore, all one can say is that the substance of the signifier is always material (sounds, objects, images)."[21] Yet this interpretation of the image carrier as signifier can be observed in Peirce and Goodman as well. Both of them mean by *image, icon,* or *representation* a flat, material object. When Peirce says that in the case of an icon there is a relation of resemblance between the "sign" (Peirce's concept for the signifier) and the "object" (his concept for the signified), he understands by "icon" a material object, since for him the icon, like all other types of signs, has a material sign body [*Zeichenkörper*].

The following sentence shows that Goodman, too, discusses the relation of resemblance between an image and the object pictured, that is, between representation and denotatum [*Denotat*], as if both terms of the relation were of a material kind: "A Constable painting of Marlborough Castle is more like any other picture than it is like the Castle."[22] This claim only makes sense if *picture* stands for image carrier: two flat, painted canvases undoubtedly resemble each other more than a canvas and a castle. We can thus see here that by *picture* Goodman means image carrier. Correspondingly, he says about an image, painted in shades of gray, of a seaside landscape: "the picture denotes a certain scene and is a concrete instance of certain shades of gray."[23] This means that what takes on the function of denotation is the canvas painted in gray; what refers when a painting refers is a painted, material surface.

There is agreement on one decisive point: all image theorists assume that, in the case of images that are used as signs, the perception of the image plays a central role in the identification of the referent. Klaus Sachs-Hombach therefore proposes for images the fitting concept "signs close to perception [*wahrnehmungsnahe Zeichen*]."[24] This idea of a dependence on perception can be found in all image theories and semiotics of the image—as in Peirce's definition of the icon: "An *Icon* is a sign which refers to the Object that it denotes merely by virtue of characters of its own, and which it possesses, just the same, whether any such Object actually exists or not."[25] Goodman, too, underscores this dependence: "To represent, a picture must function as a pictorial symbol; that is, function in a system such that what is denoted depends solely on the pictorial properties of the symbol."[26] The question that remains open, however, is simply this: what are pictorial properties? Goodman's answer is unambiguous: "A pictorial characterization may name the colors at several places, or state that the color at one place lies within a certain range, or state that the colors at two places are complementary and so on."[27]

This allows us to articulate the problem more precisely. If in the case of images that are used as signs the perception of the image is necessary for the determination of the referent, we must ask: perception of what? What do we have to look at when we have to look at an image to construct a pictorial reference? Is it a perception of the displaying image carrier or of the displayed image object that is the concern here? A suspicion imposes itself: the suspicion that no canvas whatsoever refers when images refer to castles. For these questions can be easily answered, since image carrier and image object have entirely different perceivable characteristics and are hardly confused. What we look at to operate a denotation with an image is unambiguous. It is exclusively the appearance [*Aussehen*] of the image object that is taken into consideration in the determination of the referent. In the use of the image as sign, the materiality of the image does not play any function that would determine meaning. It should be beyond dispute that images that look different can be used as signs for other things—but what is meant by *image* is exclusively the image object. The appearance of the image carrier (the computer screen, the canvas, etc.) is even overlooked in the construction of the reference relation, as the propositions common in dealing with images show: *This is not a photo of Peter because Peter looks entirely different.* What we mean by that is not that he looks entirely different from a 3.5"-x-5" piece of photo paper, as Goodman seems to think when he says that paintings resemble each other more than they do a castle.

We have arrived at the crucial point: when images denote, they do not denote the things we can determine by means of looking at the visible properties of computer screens, canvases, and photo papers, but they denote things that can be determined when we pay attention to the visible properties of the image object. If we further say that in the case of pictorial signs the denotatum is determined by means of considering the appearance of the signifier, the result is the following: in the sentence *An image denotes something*, what is meant by *image* is the image object. The use of images as signs consists in that an immaterial, which means exclusively visible, object is brought into appearance [*Erscheinung*] by means of a material image carrier and is then used as signifier. Every object can be used as a sign, even—as in the case of the image object—an object that is present only artificially. The signifier of a pictorial sign is simply no more physically present than a real dog is present by means of its image. The signifier of an image that is used as a sign changes as little over time as does a displayed dog. By means of the use of images as signs, image objects become signifiers; something is used as sign that is exclusively visible and is not subject to the laws of physics. Or, put differently, the image carrier is not the sign carrier but displays the sign carrier.

We must take seriously an idea we may perhaps be unaccustomed to—an idea that seems typical for a phenomenological semiotics of the image. Husserl leaves no doubt as to his view that the image object takes on the function of the sign carrier. Thus he writes about the image object: "By the image object we do not mean the depicted object, the *image subject*, but the precise analogue of the *phantasy image*; namely the appearing object that is the representant of the image *subject*."[28] This means that it is the image object that takes on the function of serving as a sign: "We therefore distinguish the representing image, the appearing object that possesses the depictive function and through which the image subject is depicted, from the physical image."[29] If the image is used as a sign, "the appearing object is not just taken by itself, but as the representant of another object like it or resembling it."[30] This means the resemblance between image and denotatum is a resemblance between "representing image object"[31] and represented image subject. When we confront this idea of Husserl's with the standpoint of Goodman and Peirce, it becomes clear at which point their semiotics of the image part ways: one path projects a semiotics that treats the *image carrier* as a means for symbolic representation, and the other path must lead to a semiotics that treats the *image object* as a means for symbolic representation. It is worth a try to explore this path a little more. For this purpose the question of the relation between image carrier and image object poses itself.

The enigmatic relation between image carrier and image object

If, in respect to the relation between image carrier and image object, we want to limit ourselves with philosophical skepticism to the description of certainties, we will have to agree with Ernst H. Gombrich's classical opinion that the consciousness of the image object is "a psychological effect. Such effects can be discussed, but they cannot be demonstrated."[32] The strength of this view consists in its description of the emergence of a consciousness of the image object from the viewing of an image carrier as an "unsolved psychological puzzle."[33] We must say it plainly: how an image carrier is able to produce in the viewer the consciousness of "an image object presently presenting itself"[34] is, at least for the moment, inexplicable—and that is not really peculiar, for if we had an explanation, we would have solved nothing less than one of the great enigmas of humanity. The relation between image carrier and image object is the relation between a physical and an intentional object. For this, in the end, is the decisive difference between the image carrier and the image object: one exists as a piece of the world, and the other is a nothing, not part of the world but an object for a consciousness. As a consequence, what we are concerned with in the viewing of images is the problem of how the perception of a material thing produces a certain intentional consciousness. And this means that our concern is how processes that can be described by means of physical concepts become phenomena that do not have any physical properties.

Yet what cannot be explained can at least sometimes be described more precisely. Even if we do not know how a perceived image carrier brings about the consciousness of an image object, we can still differentiate that the use of images as signs is the use of a thing displayed—by means of the image carrier—as a sign. This is not to deny that the image carrier is a necessary medial precondition for the visible-only existence of the displayed image object—but the image carrier is not used as a sign; it is used to present an image object. An image carrier must be given for an image object to become visible in the first place and for it, then, to be usable semiotically as a signifier. Yet this means that the visible givenness of the signifier does not consist in a semiotic process but in a process of perception that precedes every semiotic use. Inexplicably, the image object, and thus that which becomes a signifier in the semiotic use of the image, is visible on the image carrier. But seeing what serves as a sign is not itself a process of signification [*Zeichenprozeß*] but an optical phenomenon. That is why we have to distinguish not only image carrier and image object but equally also the different functions that these two visible aspects of the image take on in the use of images as signs. We find these two functions differentiated in Husserl: "The physical image awakens the mental image and this in turn presents something else, the subject [*Sujet*]."[35] The function of the image carrier thus consists in awakening a mental image (a synonym for the image object). "Awakening" is a particularly fitting metaphor for this activity of the image carrier: we do not know how this "awakening," precisely this coming-to-consciousness, functions. The second function is that of the image object, which consists in standing for a subject, which means "that it 'counts' not for itself but as a 'pictorial presentation' of an object that resembles it."[36] Yet this second function presupposes a success of the first act, that is a coming-to-appearance of the image object used; its visibility logically precedes its legibility. Hence, Husserl continues: "Here we must not overlook that the representing image, like any appearing object, in turn constitutes itself in an act (which act founds the pictorial character in the first place)."[37]

That something that is physically necessary for the existence of the signifier is nonetheless not a part of the signifier is not unusual at all. The very light that lights the image carrier is a physically necessary precondition for an image object to become visible—yet hardly anyone would want to say that the light functions as sign carrier when an image functions as a sign. We are dealing here with the difference between a medium and a sign. There are many media that make the presence of signifiers possible: a telephone line is one of many material preconditions for the presence of audible signifiers in a phone conversation; nonetheless, we would not address the phone line as part of the signifiers with which communication takes place in a phone conversation. And it is in this sense that the image carrier is a medium that makes image objects visible and their semiotic use possible. The image medium—the canvas, the screen, the paper—makes it possible for us to see the image object in the first place and then, in addition, to use it as a signifier. This does not change even when we note that we can use an image object as a signifier only if it is used simultaneously and jointly with an image carrier. What is decisive is that both aspects of the image, even if they are used simultaneously, are nonetheless used in entirely different ways. We let the image carrier display to us an image object that we ourselves in turn use to refer to something—the way we hear words and sentences through a telephone in order to refer to something by means of them. Yet hardly anyone wants to say that the phone's receiver was itself a symbol. The receiver actualizes the presence of symbols, but it is not a part of the signifier. And in entirely analogous fashion the image carrier, too, actualizes the signifier without being part of the signifier.

The distinction between pictorial and nonpictorial signs

One basic distinction is important for describing the use of images as signs. Every object—be it an image object or a real thing—can be used as a sign. That is why we must consider that the materially present image carrier of an image, too, can be used as a sign. Yet when an image carrier is being used for this purpose, we are dealing with a special case: we would just barely be able to say that an image was used as a sign. We must, therefore, make a distinction: images can be used as pictorial and as nonpictorial signs. This latter case is of interest to image theory mainly for reasons of completeness. The following, rather odd, cases are examples for the use of an image in the sense of using the image carrier as a nonpictorial sign.

If someone takes the bullet holes in an image as a sign for a shooting, the image carrier serves as an indication. In the case that someone sells an image at an auction in order to give a secret sign for something, he uses the image carrier as a conventional sign. These functions can also be taken on by a thing that is not an image; the image carrier is a thing. Goodman, in this context, presents the case of a briefing officer who uses the images in a commandeered museum to stand for enemy emplacements.[38] Even though the images are then used as signs, they are not used as pictorial signs.

Things become complicated, however, when we ask whether it is possible to conceive of a case of nonpictorial use of the image object. We can find an example in the widespread use of images in psychology. When psychologists look at the images drawn by children in order to find out whether these children have been treated badly or even abused and if they have suffered psychological damage, they examine exclusively the image objects. They will hardly concern themselves with the question of whether the children have drawn them with markers or crayons. If there are no special circumstances demanding it, they will not pay attention to the image carrier. They treat image objects as signs, yet not as pictorial signs but as symptoms of actions and disturbances. For we could not say that the image that allows for inferring abuse is an image of abuse; the image does not display the abuse in the way we have in mind when we say *The image displays Peter*. The image instead is taken to be an indication for the existence of abuse. This means that we have here an example for an image object being used as a sign, but not as a pictorial sign. The image object is not used to refer to a similar object, but the existence of certain image objects is taken as a symptom for the existence of certain psychological states.

Even more complicated, indeed in most cases undecidable, is the situation in the case of the pictorial presentation of symbols in the narrow sense of the term; think of Giorgione's *Sleeping Venus*. Venus, any encyclopedia will tell us, usually functions as a symbol of love—the question is just: in an image of Venus, which Venus is the symbol of love? The Venus to whom we refer by means of the image, that is, this mythological idea, or the Venus who is artificially present as image object? In the first case we could no longer say that the image—neither the image carrier nor the image object—is itself a symbol. The image would be just a pictorial sign by which we refer to something that is a symbol of love. The image of Venus by itself would be no more a symbol than a woman by herself. This decision determines how close we let the symbolic dimension of images get to us. Are the images that display symbols images that refer to symbols, or are the artificially present image objects what serve as symbols? In the second case we would be dealing with the nonpictorial use of an image object as a sign.

The use of real objects as images

The use of images as pictorial signs is certainly more decisive than the odd and complicated exceptions in which image carriers and image objects are used as nonpictorial signs. The use of images as pictorial signs can indeed be precisely defined. There is use of an image as a pictorial sign when the image object serves to identify an object that bears visible resemblance to the image object.[39] The following, then, is of particular relevance. That this kind of sign is only possible with images is in no way due to the use of resemblance for the determination of meaning but solely to the use of image objects as sign carriers—and image objects are, for better or for worse, only visible in images. When images are used as signs, they identify a reference in such a way that this reference can also be applied to real things. Every real object can also be used in the way image objects are used when they serve as pictorial signs. Real things are then used like images, yet that does not make them images. That is why it is important to consider not only the distinction between pictorial sign and nonpictorial sign but also the distinction between the use of images as pictorial signs and the use of real things as pictorial signs. A use of images as pictorial signs does not arise from turning a relation of resemblance between two things into a relation of reference (that is possible with any thing) but from using an image object as a sign in such a way. For when something is used as an image, this something does not become an image. That would only be the case if we wanted to understand the concept of the image as a functional concept. Indeed what is at stake here is the difference that the concept of the sign but not the concept of the image is a functional concept. Let the following example mark this important difference.

Somebody wants to buy a pack of screws and shows the salesperson a sample screw he has brought with him. The customer refers, by means of a present, real screw, to absent, real screws, precisely to those screws that bear a resemblance to the one he has brought with him. For Peirce this kind of use turns the screw that was brought along into an icon, which shows us that his concept of the icon is a functional concept. For it seems beyond dispute that in this example the signifier (the screw that was brought along) is put into a relation of reference with the absent screws through their resemblance. Yet beside the point that this use is dependent on context, the decisive disadvantage of this view consists in that it allows real things to become images simply by such uses. Every thing becomes an icon when it is used to refer to something to which it bears a resemblance. When someone shows a salesperson a screw and says *Please bring me similar screws,* there is, to be sure, construction of a reference, a construction that takes into consideration a resemblance, yet the screw does not, by virtue of this use, become an image. For if the screw were to be addressed as an image on the basis of this use, we would not consider it to be important that in this case the image of a screw is itself a screw. Yet precisely this characteristic, at least from a phenomenological point of view, is not negotiable: images display something that they themselves are not. That is why we cannot define the concept of the image functionally as long as we demand of images that they possess certain characteristics, namely an iconic difference, an antagonistic difference between image carrier and image object. Images do not become images by means of resemblance but only by means of displaying things that are not subject to the laws of physics. The nonphysical image objects might then bear resemblances to other things, like all objects—but no resemblance is sufficient for pictoriality. Hence, when an object is used semiotically like an image, we should not take the extra step and, for this reason, call this object an image—precisely in opposition to a sign! For in the case of signs it is indeed true that everything that is used as a sign really is a sign as well. That the concept of the sign but not the concept of the image can be defined functionally is a difference whose consideration can make many discussions more precise—for example when we wonder, like Hilary Putnam, whether ants can draw images: "An ant is crawling on a patch of sand. As it crawls, it traces a line in the sand. By pure chance the line that it traces curves and recrosses itself in such a way that it ends up looking like a recognizable caricature of Winston Churchill. Has the ant traced an image of Winston Churchill, an image that depicts Churchill?"[40] Putnam is right to claim that it would be absurd to suppose that the ant has created an image that would refer to Churchill. Yet when Putnam argues that this trace cannot be an image of Churchill because this trace cannot refer to Churchill, he wrongly presupposes that images always refer to that which bears resemblance to what they display as image object. Putnam does not distinguish between image and representation. His ant on the beach has created something that may not have the properties of an image for ants but may have them for humans: an image object is visible. This image is not used by its producer as a sign for anything (and probably cannot be used as such by ants). This example shows that the production of an artificial presence of something is a capacity of images that can, by chance, also be brought about by animals. Animals, too, can create things that for humans have the properties of images—yet animals can create neither depictions nor imitations. For depiction as much as imitation presupposes an intention. Indeed, Putnam's example allows us to differentiate the concepts of "imitation," "depiction," and "image."

That the ant has created neither a pictorial imitation nor a depiction of Churchill is due to the fact that in opposition to images, imitations and depictions as such must be produced on purpose. Similar to the way in which an image does not have to be a sign but can be a sign, an image can be an imitation but does not have to be.[41] An imitation that comes about by chance is inconceivable—the same is true for a sign come about by chance—but images that come about by chance can be conceived. In this respect we can determine a clear relation between imitations and images: there are images that are imitations, but not every image is an imitation. The traces of the ant are an image in which we see an image object that bears a resemblance to Churchill, but the ant has drawn neither a pictorial imitation nor a depiction of Churchill. Imitations or depictions are produced consciously and, in most cases, are consciously used as signs for something. From this perspective there might very well be images that come about by chance, but there are no depictions that come about by chance. The traces of the ant are an image that presents something that by chance bears a resemblance to Churchill. It is possible to use the image made by the ant as a pictorial sign for Churchill—yet in all probability this can only be done by human beings.

That there is a relation of resemblance between the signifier and the signified (or denotatum) is in no way specific to pictorial signs. There are nonpictorial signs as well in whose case the signified bears a resemblance to the signifier. We can only speak of a pictorial sign if the signifier—in addition to the use that considers resemblance—is produced with an image, if an image object is used that is visible beforehand, even independently of its use as a sign. That is why we are dealing with a completely different situation when the customer shows the salesperson an image of a screw. In that case the customer no longer refers with a real screw to absent real screws but refers with an artificially present screw to absent real screws. He uses a screw that he displays, that is, an image object, to refer to things. He does the same with an image object that he would have done with real screws. Yet when he uses the image object as a sign, he uses as a sign a thing that exists thanks only to a carrier and exists in a visible way and only for the viewer as object of his present perception. In short, an image is used as a sign precisely if the image object is used as a sign and namely if the denotatum (as Goodman calls it) or the image subject (as Husserl calls it) is determined by the appearance [*Aussehen*] of the image object. This explains why it is only in the case of images that a closer look can determine more precisely the *meaning* of the pictorial sign. But it may be the case that a closer look at the screws the customer brings along can help to determine more precisely what screws are to be bought. In the case of images this is common usage. In the use of images as signs, the things, to which the image then refers, are determined by means of the appearance of the image object. No image object by itself is able to determine a denotatum—as Husserl notes with exceptional clarity: "The image object does not refer to anything; that is, to anything the way a symbol does. It does not point away from itself, does not point outward, even if toward something similar that would present itself as different from what already appears in the image."[42] Images are signs if a relation is established by means of the image object—but this reference does not arise simply from the appearance of the image object, for if we look at an image object, we still have to know what to pay attention to. We must have a rule of application about how the image object is to refer. The viewer must know the sense of the image in order to be able to identify a denotatum by means of observing an image object.

The sense of an image

An image object can be used for pictorial reference only if the viewer of the image object is familiar with a rule that describes how a reference to an object can be constructed by means of the appearance [*Aussehen*] of this image object. We can call this rule the sense of an image. The sense is thus the preconception about how an object is to be identified by means of the visible image object. Because in the case of the sense we are dealing with a rule, it is impossible for the sense to be visible in the image itself; rules, in principle, cannot be visible. The sense is brought to the image. It is not a visible property of either the image carrier or the image object but precisely the rule whose application leads to our ability to refer by means of the image object to one or more objects, even if we do not in fact do so or if we cannot do so because the reference object does not exist. If we suppose that image objects, because they bear a visible resemblance to other real things, do not automatically refer to these, then something must be added to the image object such that its resemblance to something is discovered and used for a reference. Since the image object serves as a signifier, the appearance of the image carrier does not play any role in the identification of the meaning of the image. The following example is particularly well suited to explain the sense of an image and its role in the use of an image as a sign.

Think of a photograph that is used as a sign for a person. Propositions are articulated about this photograph such as *This is an image of Woody Allen* or *This image denotes Woody Allen*. These propositions tell us that the image is used to refer to something that bears a resemblance to the image object visible in the image. This resemblance is insufficient for a reference to emerge, yet this does not preclude the construction of a reference by means of resemblance. In a portrait this reference to a concrete person can be produced by giving the image the sense of referring the image object that becomes visible on the image carrier to a person who resembles it. This sense is a contingent and conventional ascription that cannot be taken from the image itself. It is the sense typical of portraits. It is indeed by no means the case that every image that is used as a sign has a specific sense. The sense of the image, rather, is a conventional rule that is used for a conventionally fixed group of images—for that group of images, precisely, that have the same sense. What is decisive is that this group is formed without regard to the technique by which the images of this group were produced. Portraits have the same sense, independently of whether they are photographs, prints, oil paintings, or films. Because the sense of an individual image, most of the time, is given by the image's belonging to a group of images, we can know the sense of an image even if we do not yet know the individual image. Portraits are such a group of images that have the same sense, namely to denote the person who can be determined by means of the appearance of the image object. That is why we can say that only if we know the sense can we determine a denotatum by means of the appearance of an image object. This does not mean, however, that this denotatum must really exist. Portraits can serve as an example of this as well: there are fictional portraits. This shows us: should we want to define portraits such that they are the image of a real person, then there could by definition be no fictional portraits. Yet portraits do not necessarily have a real person as their denotatum. They only have the sense of being used for determining people. These people, however, do not have to exist. We can ascribe sense to an image that can be referred only to a made-up person. That is why a portrait of a man from Mars is conceivable. In that case we would be dealing with a—Goodman's fitting concept offers itself—"null denotation."[43] The image denotes something that does not exist. Yet an image that denotes a thing that does not exist is used differently from an image looked at without a sense. In the case of the null denotation the denoted object does not really exist but exists only as a possibility: with this sense the image could be used to denote a person who does not exist.

If the same image object is looked at with a different sense, this same image object becomes usable as a pictorial sign for other things. That is why the same image that in one context has the sense of denoting a person can be used in a different context and with a different sense to denote a different object. If the portrait of Woody Allen were part of a catalog for glasses, the context would intimate that the sense of the image consists in referring with the image object to the glasses, which glasses can be determined by means of the appearance of the image object. The same image object is used to refer to a pair of glasses that could also be referred to Woody Allen. Yet this is only possible if in each case we are familiar with the sense—if we know, for example, that images in sales catalogs have the sense of referring to things sold by the company that publishes the catalog. That is why we also know, by means of this sense, that we are to refer with the pair of glasses visible in the image not to that concrete pair of glasses Woody Allen had on his nose when the photo was taken. The image in the catalog denotes the model of glasses or maybe even a company's entire collection of glasses. Switching the photo from a catalog for glasses over into a catalog for sweaters already changes the sense and, as a consequence, the denotation.

This example makes it clear that the context of the appearance [*Erscheinungskontext*] determines to a high degree with which sense the viewer will use the image as a sign. This is also true for photographs about which it is often claimed that their reference is not dependent on a contingent use since there exists a causal relation between photographs and their denotatum. But here, too, we must consider the following: an image object can never be causally connected with the object for which it is used as a pictorial sign, since an image object is not an object in the physical world at all but an object that exclusively appears visibly. Nonetheless, we can look at an image object with the sense of using it as a sign for one of the many objects of which the image carrier, on which the image object appears to the beholder, is, among other things, a physical trace. Such a sense leads to a photo of Woody Allen's being used to denote Woody Allen, for in such a photo Woody Allen, by means of a photochemical process, has caused the image carrier to appear in such a way that we are convinced we see on it something that bears a resemblance to Woody Allen. Yet the fact that the image carrier is a fixed light trace of the real Woody Allen by itself is no reason for the image object that resembles Woody Allen to automatically and unconditionally refer symbolically to the causative, real Woody Allen. Quite the opposite: a completely different use of image objects in photographs is rather common. When photographs present image objects, these image objects, like in every other image's case, can be used as pictorial signs according to the ascription of sense for all things that can be identified by means of the image objects' appearance; the denotata can participate, in a physical sense, in the production [*Entstehung*] of the image carrier, but they do not have to. As soon as the title *Zelig* is placed underneath a photograph of Woody Allen, we will use the visible image object (which could still well be used as a pictorial sign for Woody Allen) as a sign for a different, in this case fictional, person. This photo then denotes Zelig in the same way a painting of Zelig could. The photograph would be a null denotation, for it refers to a fictional person even though a real person was photographed for the production of the photograph. This shows us that the photo taken of a thing does not have to be used for the denotation of that thing. In the situation of the Zelig image it would therefore make sense to say that the photo of Woody Allen serves as a pictorial sign for the purpose of denoting Zelig. For "photo of Woody Allen" simply says that a light trace of Woody Allen is fixed chemically.[44] That is why it is not surprising that a photograph of a person can also be used as a sign for another real person, which is always the case when an actor plays the part of a real person. This employment of images is particularly widespread in movies. In most cases even, films are not used as pictorial signs for the filmed actors but as pictorial signs for completely different people who did not stand in front of the camera at all. This is true, however, not only of actors: a photo can denote a real house, even if in reality the photo is taken of cardboard scenery. Whether we take an image to be a sign for an actor or as a sign for the person depicted by the actor is determined exclusively by the sense that is fixed by the title and the context or is assumed for some other reason by the viewer. In a biography of Woody Allen we could once more refer the image already mentioned, which was previously used as a sign for Zelig, to Woody Allen; then, perhaps, the caption would read *Woody Allen in* Zelig, *1983*.

The difference between a photo of someone and an image as a sign for someone becomes clear when we think of identical twins, one of whom has her image taken. The result is a photo of a twin that can well be used as a pictorial sign for either twin. Even if this kind of employment contradicts the widespread sense of a photograph, what is solely decisive for the functional principle of pictorial signs is that this kind of use of the photo as a pictorial sign is possible and will work without problems. It is conceivable that each twin has a photograph of the other glued in her passport. This could happen on purpose but also because of a mishap. The twins would each have a wrong *photo*, for the image carrier is not a trace of the passport holder, but a correct *image* in their passports, for the image can be used as a sign to identify the holder of the passport. In the context of portraits of people this distinction of photograph and image may sound idiosyncratic. Yet in catalogs it is perfectly common usage to show a product with photographs even though the customer can in no way buy the same object that was photographed, only an identical object for which the photo is used as a pictorial sign. In a different context, for example on the Web site of an antiques dealer who sells originals and unique pieces, in contrast, the images will be used as signs for precisely those objects that were photographed with the camera. What does this show? The image in a car catalog is used as a sign with a different sense from the image in the antiques catalog. Yet in all cases it remains true that while the photograph is referred as a pictorial sign to one of the objects that participated in causing the appearance of the image carrier, this is a sense that, however typical of photographs it might be, is contingent for all of them as well; it is a sense that determines the use of images as signs only in certain contexts. The image objects of photographs, too, can be used as pictorial signs for every object that bears a resemblance to the image object; the place in which they appear and the title usually provide the rule to which of the many possible objects that bear a resemblance to the image object the image is to be referred in a concrete case.

We can deduce a hermeneutic generalization from these examples: an image's unknown sense can be determined by means of searching for the question that can be answered by looking at the image object. For if the sense of an image is a rule with which we can refer an image object to a thing, then it must be possible to delimit this sense by determining the questions that can be answered by looking at the image object. This tells us that the sense of an image must enable the viewer to refer by means of the image object and by reason of its appearance to a group of things. Since we must be able to expect this capacity from the sense of an image, there are limits fixed by the image object as to what can be the sense of an image. The sense fixes *how* an image object is to be used as a sign. The image object, however, fixes *what* can be its sense. It makes sense only for the rule of application to be the sense of an image, a rule that makes it possible for the image object to refer to something by reason of its appearance. Imagine a landscape painting had a title that passed it off as the portrait of a particular person. In this case the title would ascribe a sense to the image that the image cannot redeem: it is not possible to identify a particular person by means of a landscape painting. A general principle of exclusion derives from this negation: since the possibilities of ascribing sense have to conform to what is visible as image object, we can, conversely, speculate hermeneutically about a possible intended sense. Such speculation is possible if for a particular image we do not know, thanks to context or title or other indications, if and what sense is assigned to it by others. This speculation takes the form of asking what question can be satisfactorily answered by a semiotic use of the image. Finding an image without knowing with which sense it is to be used semiotically is anything but a rare occurrence. Just think of images discovered from foreign or lost cultures or of unintelligible works of art. If the sense of an image is unknown, a sense that is at least possible can be determined by asking what question this image could answer. This principle of searching for a sense supposes purposiveness: an image that can well fulfill a particular sense will be ascribed this sense. Yet that should never make us overlook that every assignment of sense is contingent: not only can it be different; it does not have to be at all. Every speculation about a possible sense can be dismissed. For every image we can look for a sense that makes it usable as a pictorial sign. Yet before this ends up auguring hermeneutic suppositions, an image may perhaps better be looked at without sense.

Looking at images without supposing a sense

What is true for all visible objects is also true for image objects: they can be looked at without their being transformed into a sign simply by reason of being looked at. The reason for this kind of viewing is by no means idiosyncratic: we look at the image object because we want to know what it looks like. Just as we can count how many windows a real house has, we can count how many windows there are on the side of a house that is shown in an image object that looks like a house—on Sartre's imaginary houses mentioned in the previous chapter, for instance. In this case we do not count the windows of an absent real house but merely visible windows. Real things are very often looked at simply because somebody wants to know what something looks like. That is why it is not really surprising that things that are displayed, too, can be looked at for the sake of their visibility—especially since we can see something in images that we cannot see outside of them. Images in principle always show something unreal, for they always show something that does not grow older; they always show something that is liberated from the constraints of physics. In contrast, without images we could only see things that are subject to the laws of physics. That is why the image medium opens up a world of new visible things: something becomes visible that does not behave according to the laws described by physics. Every image allows for a glance into a nonphysical zone.

It is precisely this property of each and every image to present [*vorstellen*] something without this something being physically present that is traditionally described by formulations such as *The image displays things that are not present* or *The image displays something it itself is not*. These definitions are ambiguous. They could be understood such that in every image a reference is given, for if the display of something that is not present is a display of something that is somewhere else, then it also follows inevitably that in every pictorial display a relation to this absent thing is produced. And the production of such a relation of reference to something absent is indeed a capacity only signs have. Winfried Nöth argues that the phenomenological position is "hard to follow already on the basis of everyday speech, for how can it be that something 'displays [*zeigt*] what it itself is not' and in so doing is not a sign [*Zeichen*]?"[45] The problem with this argument is that it assumes that the display of something that is not present corresponds to the display of something that is somewhere else—this identity, however, is in no way a necessary one. Rather, it is important to note that "not being present" is not at all synonymous with "being absent." Hardly anyone wants to define images like this: "Images display things that are absent." If something is displayed by means of an image, this something does not have to be absent, but this something is not present; that is, it is not quite, that is, again, it is not completely, present. For it is indeed exclusively visibly present and not present in that complete way accessible to all senses with which we are familiar from real things. The image object is not not in attendance because it is absent but because it has no real existence; the image object exists for the viewer—to take up a terminological distinction of Dieter Mersch's—in an "attendance without presence [*Anwesenheit ohne Gegenwart*]."[46] It appears to the viewer in its kind of existence not like a real thing because it is exclusively visible and cannot be heard, smelled, touched, or tasted. Yet we expect this accessibility to all senses from things that materially exist, are present and in attendance. An image object, however, cannot offer this, which is why it is not quite present [*gegenwärtig*] but precisely merely artificially present [*artifiziell präsent*], that is, reduced to visibility. We could also say that the proposition *An image displays something it itself is not* means *The image carrier displays an image object and is not itself an image object*. This artificially present image object, entirely like every other real thing, can be looked at without sense and meaning as well. This is possible—even if we, like Edmund Husserl for example, may think of such a looking at images without semiotic usage, a looking reduced to perception, as unusual and perfectly abnormal.

Indeed, Husserl takes an idiosyncratic stance on looking at images without semiotic usage. To be sure, he describes very precisely that the appearing image object can be looked at without thereby already having to function as a sign: "With the constitution of this appearance, however, the relation to the image *subject* has not yet been constituted."[47] Yet for Husserl this possibility—compared to the way of dealing with images he is familiar with—is purely theoretical and devoid of normalcy: "With a simple apprehension, therefore, we would not yet have any image at all in the proper sense, but at most the object that subsequently functions as an image."[48] We can see that Husserl is caught up in a contradiction: on the one hand he is persuaded by the traditional understanding of the image according to which the image is and must be a figurative image [*Abbild*] of a real thing: "If the conscious relation to something depicted is not given with the image, then we certainly do not have an image."[49] In "normal phantasy presentation and image presentation,"[50] the viewer orients him- or herself toward the image subject. Yet on the other hand, Husserl's distinction between image object and physical image, as well as his thesis that the presenting image object functions as a representative, forces him to suppose that it must be possible to look at images as mere presentations without sign character [*Zeichenhaftigkeit*]. For Husserl assumes that the consciousness of the image object is inexplicably awoken by the physical image carrier, that this "nonthing supposedly appearing to us as present"[51] is not a symbol on its own but that it merely can *function* as a symbol—yet when it does not do so, it is still visible. As quoted above: "The image object does not refer to anything; that is, to anything the way a symbol does. It does not point away from itself, does not point outward, even if toward something similar that would present itself as different from what already appears in the image."[52]

The logic of his own description of the image forces on Husserl an idea he dislikes. In this regard he compares the content of phantasy with the image object: "Now the figment, just like ordinary pictoriality by means of pictorialization, can represent something that resembles it." The decisive word is *can*, for it is because of this that Husserl has to continue: "Of course, one would also have to consider the possibility that it represents nothing further at all, but is taken simply as it is, presenting nothing beyond itself."[53] Despite his sympathies for the traditional understanding of the image, which in his opinion amounts to the normal understanding, he sketches the perspective of an asemiotic viewing of images, a perspective he immediately wants to marginalize as an aesthetic problem: "We have to distinguish intuitive image consciousness, the consciousness that belongs to immanent pictoriality, from the *images* that function as *symbols* and from the image consciousness that comes about in the symbolic function of the image. The consciousness belonging to immanent pictoriality alone plays a role in the *aesthetic contemplation of the image.*"[54] This intimation is all there is, yet it does allow us to discern a direction. At the very least we get the impression that Husserl understands the aesthetic viewing of images in the literal sense as a viewing that concentrates on perception, as the attempt to look at only the internal, immanent properties of the image object. If this is the idea, then every kind of using the image as a symbol would be precluded—and this means not only the use of the image for denotation but equally its use for exemplification, which is often seen as a form of symbolization specific to aesthetic works. For images that denote and exemplify are used by the viewer not just aesthetically, not just perceptively, but already symbolically. In this respect exemplification is only a special case of denotation—albeit a very remarkable one that is worth a more precise description, one that considers the difference between image carrier and image object.

Exemplification with image carriers and
image objects

One particular kind of sense assignation that happens to aesthetic objects in particular consists in using an object to refer to properties this object itself possesses. Nelson Goodman points out this special yet by no means uncommon kind of self-referential denotation and calls it "exemplification." What seems decisive is that exemplification is only a particular kind of denotation. For exemplification, too, is a reference to something—albeit in the case of exemplification this something is a property of the thing that is used as a sign. Exemplification can be defined as follows: "An object that is literally or metaphorically denoted by a predicate, and refers to that predicate or the corresponding property, may be said to exemplify that predicate or property."[55] We must, therefore, distinguish two kinds of exemplification, namely literal and metaphorical.

Yet in the case of the special form that is the self-referential denotation of properties of the image, once again we have the problem that we would like to know what exactly is meant by "image" when we speak of the exemplifying image. The problem in the application of this idea to images is their "double objecthood [*doppelte Gegenständlichkeit*]":[56] "The ordinary image then is not a simple, but a double fact."[57] What is meant is that an image possesses both a real presence as image carrier and an artificial presence as image object. If an image is given, there are two objects that appear differently; they are there not in the same way but to the same extent. Accordingly each of these two objects can be used for exemplification. When we consider that the concept "image" in the sentence *An image can exemplify metaphorically and literally* can mean both image object and image carrier, we see that not two but at least four forms of exemplification have to be differentiated since both the image carrier and the image object can each be used for exemplification both literally and metaphorically. These four cases can be clarified with the following examples:

1. The use of the image carrier for literal exemplification. The photos on the counter of a photo shop, most of the time, are used for the image carriers literally to exemplify their properties. The salesperson says, "We can develop such images for you." *Image* means the image carrier, for it is the image carrier that has the properties referred to by the sample image. A concrete image carrier with certain properties refers to precisely these properties, for example when a semigloss photo is used to exemplify what semigloss prints will look like. This kind of exemplification, according to Goodman, is the only possible case of a literal exemplification with images. This is perfectly consistent for him to claim, for it is possible to say that if "image" and "image carrier" are used synonymously, we must also hold that "an image literally exemplifies only pictorial properties."[58]

2. The use of the image object for literal exemplification. If someone, in a report on fighting child pornography, shows a short excerpt from the seized photographic and film material, then this excerpt is used to exemplify how repulsive and disgusting those miserable efforts are. The images displayed make reference to properties that they literally have themselves. The individual, displayed images are themselves literally repulsive in the truest sense of the word and are used as signs for this property. What is meant by "images" in the last sentence are the image objects displayed— the motifs: the image carrier itself, in the case of these images, is not repulsive.

A further example for the use of image objects for literal exemplification would be a perspectival image that denotes properties of perspectivally constructed image objects. Think of Masaccio's famous image of the Trinity in Florence's Santa Maria Novella. Probably not the least of the intentions in its making and of its actual uses was the exemplification of what a perspectively constructed image object looks like. The image object, then, is used to make reference to properties it itself possesses: the image object, which looks [*aussieht*] spatial, refers to its own spatial appearance [*Aussehen*]. Think also of a computer game in which players race cars. The driving properties of each racecar can be adjusted; each of the simulated cars can exemplify its particular driving properties. What is used here for referring to its own literal properties is a special kind of image object, namely a virtual object.

3. The use of the image carrier for metaphorical exemplification. According to Goodman an image painted in shades of gray that is used to refer to a metaphorical property of gray paint, namely sadness, would be the familiar example par excellence for a use of the image carrier for metaphorical exemplification. The photos in a glossy sales catalog by means of their glossy, expensive, and flawless paper exemplify in a metaphorical sense the splendor and perfect industrial quality of the company that is advertising. What exemplifies in this case is the image carrier.

4. *The use of the image object for metaphorical exemplification.* Imagine a photo that displays a rainy, desolate area. This image could be used to exemplify in a metaphorical sense a sad state. The visible rain and the dull landscape themselves look sad. The image thus exemplifies something that it, in a metaphorical sense, is itself. What is meant by "image" in the last sentence is the disconsolate image object displayed.

These examples make it clear that the dichotomy of literal and metaphorical exemplification becomes a tetrachotomy when we consider the distinction between image carrier and image object. Yet such a conceptual distinction does not exclude that one and the same image (in the sense of the unity of image carrier and image object) is being used for several kinds of symbolization at a time. What makes all of this even more complicated, however, is less that an image is used for several kinds of exemplification at a time but rather that another, a fifth form of exemplification, is possible; this fifth form, even though it is particularly complicated to describe, is particularly widespread: the use of images for the exemplification of ways of seeing.

The exemplification of ways of seeing

The exemplification of ways of seeing is a form of reference by means of image objects in which—in opposition to the four forms just named—the exemplification is dependent on a preceding denotation. The exemplification of ways of seeing is the exemplification of a mode of seeing a denotatum. Especially from images taken from the history of art, we are familiar with the use of images as symbols for the ways in which they display visible objects. We may very well say that for a good number of images in the history of art, the meaning of the image lies precisely in the way in which a thing is displayed. These images exemplify a pictorial interpretation of the visible world. This particular kind of exemplification can be described by an example.

Think of one among the many famous paintings by Francesco Guardi in which he depicts the Doge's Palace in Venice. These paintings—just as a normal postcard from Venice—can be used as a pictorial denotation of this palace. If we endow the image with the sense of referring to the architectonic building, which can be determined by means of the appearance of the image object, we use the image as a denotation of this one Doge's Palace. We thus construct a relation of reference from the relation of resemblance between image object and palace. The resemblance consists in the image object and the palace having some identical visible properties; this identity concerns in particular form and arrangement, color and proportions. Yet what do we do with the differences? What is similar is also different. The appearance [*Aussehen*] of the image object is in no way identical to the appearance of the palace, nor can it be, for in that case the image object would not be an image object at all but a real palace or at least an indiscernible imitation of the palace. If the viewer were convinced that he or she saw the very same thing in the image, then he or she would be convinced he or she saw a real house and not an image object. In many respects the image object looks different—and that is not surprising. Image objects in principle look different from actual objects, for they are not really present at all but are only artificially present, and this is the difference the viewer of the image, who will hardly confuse an image object with a real object, sees. Images always look nonphysical and unreal; they look their part; they are not real objects. Yet this is a difference that exists between every image object and every real object. In order to observe this difference, we do not need to look at any particular image. In addition, however, there are specific differences in the appearance of particular image objects. Every house in an image always also looks different from the real house in a particular way. The image object always appears [*erscheint*] in a particular style.

The style of an image object becomes particularly distinct if several images are compared that have one thing in common, that they can be used as signs for the same thing—for example several images of the Doge's Palace in different styles. Guardi's image object has visible properties we could call painterly, very optical, almost early impressionist. We can easily imagine the same building depicted from the same spot in many different styles in one image each—and a visit to an image gallery offers itself to assist us in this eidetic variation. What is remarkable is that in the use of the image object as sign, we do not consider these differences of style.

The Doge's Palace by Guardi and the postcard of this building can be used to the same extent as a pictorial sign for the same palace. In the use of different image objects for the denotation of one and the same object we ignore their differences of style. If an ascribed sense makes it possible to construct a reference to a denotatum by means of the image object's appearance, then the rest of the appearance of the image object, which was not considered in the construction, has no role to play. In denotation the style of an image object is symbolically unimportant. Yet this does not preclude symbolic use of the style itself.

The formal properties of image objects can be used for the exemplification of ways of seeing. Yet this is possible only if the image object stands in a relation of reference to a denotatum. Only an image object that serves for denoting something can also exemplify an interpretation of this object. This is the decisive point: when an image object is referred to a denotatum, the image object's style can be interpreted as an interpretation of the denotatum's appearance. Because the style history of the image is the style history of denoting images, we in most cases interpret the style differences in the image's history as precisely such interpretations. Only in this way do comparisons of image and world come about, and this results in the interpretation of style as a way of seeing an object. The image object must be referred to the world in order for its kind of appearance to become a way of seeing, an explanation, or an interpretation of the world—and this is precisely what happens in the exemplification of a way of seeing by means of an image object. The image object gives an example of how a real visible object to which the image object is referred can be interpreted by means of a visible image object. The difference thus becomes the symbolic expression of an interpretation of the visible world—but that does not have to be the case.

Formal differences are not by themselves symbolic differences in the exemplification of ways of seeing; formal differences do not have to be used for the exemplification of a way of seeing. We could also simply say that image objects' differences in style do not express different interpretations of the visible world but that differences in style produce different image objects. Say we took Sartre seriously; he is convinced, after all, that the painter "creates an imaginary house on the canvas and not a sign of a house."[59] It would then be obvious that we would have to treat the differences in style of imaginary houses like we do differences in style in the history of architecture: that is, not as the result of an interpretation of a common object of reference that, in the end, is always the world. The differences in style of buildings, then, are not differences in the interpretation of a denotatum. This architectonic view is also possible of image objects. If we refer image objects not to the visible world, if we, so to speak, take a look back from virtual reality on the history of the fine arts, then differences in style become differences in the design of different things: Guardi was the architect of imaginary houses different from Giotto's. From this asemantic perspective images become an opportunity for constructing things that are merely visible and yet concrete.

The proposition *The image is an interpretation* does not, like the proposition *The image is red*, determine a property of the image object but describes a use of the image object. Only image objects that are referred by someone to something can exemplify ways of seeing this referent: no image by itself interprets the world. One interpretation that is widespread in the history of art and engages the question which object, which story, or which idea is interpreted by an image, must assume that no image is ontologically—so to speak visibly—an interpretation of anything but rather that images are always turned into an interpretation of the world by use alone. When we ask what an image exemplifies, denotes, or interprets, we must also ask who uses an image for exemplification, denotation, or interpretation. A proposition such as *Monet in this image interprets the appearance of Rouen Cathedral* is a shortened formulation that is to be spelled out as *The image by Monet can be used to display a stylized interpretation of Rouen Cathedral*. And indeed quite a few images in the history of art lend themselves to exemplifying a way of seeing the visible world. Yet even this does not change anything. That an image was made for this semiotic purpose is something we can only know; it might have been the intention of the artist, might have been a widespread usage, might be a meaningful supposition and even advantageous—and yet we cannot find a sense or a meaning in an image simply by the look of it.

We may conduct a thought experiment here. Imagine we were supposed to reconstruct as a sculpture the object, for example a person or a house, who or which was painted in a picture by Giotto or Guardi. There would then be two possibilities for how to solve this problem. We could, first, produce the sculpture in such a way that it looks like the person or the house to which or to whom the image object can be referred. We would produce a small or big copy [*Imitat*] of the real Doge's Palace or perhaps a wax figure of the person in question—that is, copies of the objects for which the image objects can be used as pictorial signs. What is decisive is this: it is no longer possible to discern in these copies the style in which the thing in the world in question was painted. Second, however, we could construct a sculpture that looks stylistically like the image object. We would then have to try to construct an object that looks like an image object painted by Guardi or Giotto. The goal would be to give to the image object the physical materiality that, as image object, it does not have. In the ideal case we would have to be able to take a photo of this sculpture that could no longer be distinguished from a photo of the painting; it must not be possible to see in the photos whether it was the reconstructed object or the painting that was photographed. If we solve the problem in this second way, we interpret the style of the painting not as the interpretation of a visible reality but as the creation [*Gestaltung*] of a visible object—of an object, however, that is not really but, since we are dealing with an image object, only artificially present. Especially since the classics of the history of art are rarely dealt with this way, the fact that little plastic sculptures are so often produced of comic figures in precisely this sense is an indication that comic images most of the time are not used in such a way as to stylistically interpret the visible world but in such a way that in a panel the image's style serves to present objects that themselves have this style. The style is then understood not as the exemplification of a way of seeing but as the design of an object or, put more precisely, as the design of the image object. The image used this way enlarges the world of visible things but not in the sense that the image displayed something interpreted stylistically, something that would really be visible in another location without this style. Rather, the image inserts into the world of visible things a new visible architecture that, without images, does not exist in this stylistic quality: constructed image objects. The world, in this case, is not newly interpreted by images, but the world is populated with things by means of images; there is an increase in being—an idea that is relevant not least of all to the abstract images of concrete photography.

What Could "Abstract Photography" Be?

We have two ways to think about abstract photography, a topic that has not been studied sufficiently. These possibilities are distinct—albeit, most of the time, just implicitly—in the way they put the question. We can ask *What is abstract photography?* but also *What could "abstract photography" be?* These are two markedly different ways of thinking about abstract photography, and we have to differentiate.

The first question, *What is abstract photography?*, is concerned with empirical matters of fact. There are objects that can be subsumed under the concept "abstract photography," a concept probably first used programmatically by Alvin Langdon Coburn in 1916.[1] When we ask, *What is abstract photography?*, we want to study these objects in more detail, for example their particular properties or their miscellaneous variations. We want to know who made these things and when; perhaps we also want to know why they are called what they are called. We will quickly notice that a competent answer to the question *What is abstract photography?* can only be given by someone who is familiar with its history and contemporary practice, presumably a historian of art or of photography. The criterion of whether the historian gives a right or a wrong, a good or a bad, answer will always be created by the facts. The answers are measured by whether they correspond to reality—whatever we may mean by that.[2]

The second question, *What could "abstract photography" be?*, is asked much more rarely. It is concerned in principle with possibilities of thought and is thus categorically distinct from the first question. It is therefore hardly answered by empirical or historical knowledge but primarily by variations in fantasy and logical argumentation. This is obvious, for the question *What could "abstract photography" be?* is no longer concerned with the description of empirical realities but with the discovery of conceivable possibilities; it is concerned with the *concept* of abstract photography. The problem has shifted: what is foregrounded is not what something is but what something could be. In this respect the history and current practice of abstract photography can at best be a tool in getting to know possibilities of abstract photography—guided by the simple principle that what is actual must also be possible. Yet conversely—and this is decisive—we cannot find in actuality an overview of the totality of possibilities. There is no guarantee whatsoever that everything that is possible has been made actual. Empirical actuality can therefore no longer be the criterion by which we judge whether the question concerning the conceivable variations [*Ausgestaltungsformen*] abstract photography could create is answered correctly or wrongly, well or badly. When we are concerned with the possibilities of interpreting a concept, only logical soundness, imagination [*Vorstellungskraft*], and completeness determine the value of our arguments. That is why we are dealing with a question that is no longer primarily discussed in art history but in philosophy and in artists' programmatic statements. These, at least, are the typical places for experimenting with possibilities of thought and making them explicit. When we deal with possibilities of thought, attention is no longer directed to what is meant by a concept but to the concept itself. In the end, when we ask *What could "abstract photography" be?*, we study the sense of a concept, and in this concern we encounter the intention of numerous aesthetics or programs written by artists. For artists share this with the philosopher: they are less interested in the present works of their colleagues than they are in new, unknown, as yet not elaborated possibilities of this kind of photography. That is why the answer to the question *What could "abstract photography" be?* may well enter the realm of the visionary and the utopian.

The questions *What is abstract photography?* and *What could "abstract photography" be?* should not be played off one another; they are not an alternative. Neither question is the right or even the "real" one. We may, personally, consider answering one of the two questions to be important, but answering one question can in no case replace working on the other. Since the question *What is abstract photography?* in particular has been answered convincingly according to the criteria named above, it is well worth an attempt to turn, for once, to the question *What could "abstract photography" be?*

The concepts "abstract" and "photography"

In the composite "abstract photography," the adjective *abstract* serves the purpose of determining a particular form of photography. Fortunately, it is beyond debate that this closer determination is meant in the sense of a classification and not in that of an evaluation. The adjective *abstract* is not used to evaluate but to describe. The concept "abstract photography" is therefore of a completely different nature than are, for example, the concepts "political photography," "beautiful photography," or "creative photography." For what is political, beautiful, or creative depends to a high degree on conceptions of morality, norms, and values. That is why it is not possible to discern in the photograph itself whether it is political, beautiful, or creative. Yet this is precisely what is not to be the case for abstract photography. The abstract is a classification without any evaluation that is oriented toward specific properties of this kind of photograph—and these properties, precisely, are what we have to determine.

The concept "photography," taken in the widest sense, denotes the processes that produce permanent images by means of optical systems and the action of electromagnetic rays, especially of light, on materials that react to this effect. Photographically produced products are always traces that can be explained physically and chemically. Photographs are what they are on the basis of relations of cause and effect: they are the permanently visible result of manipulated radiation. So much for the wider meaning of the concept. A much more narrow sense of "photography" understands it as the technical production of figurative images of a thing by means of the optical transformation and conservation of traces of light. In this narrow sense of photography, it is primarily determined by its relation to an object, a relation based on resemblance: photography produces calculable images of visible objects.

We can distinguish between a wide and narrow meaning of the concept "abstract" as well. In the most general terms the concept "abstract" indicates that something is independent, detached, and without association. The property of being abstract is a property of precisely those phenomena that arise from abstraction. In this very wide sense of "abstract" there is no indication of what has been detached from what. Thus Hegel, for example, calls a concept abstract if it is thought without associating it with other concepts. In the much more narrow yet also much more common meaning of the concept "abstract," however, that which is abstracted from is unambiguously defined: something is abstract if it does not bear any relation to visible, concrete objects. Abstraction, then, is no longer a disregard of anything whatsoever but a disregard of a discernible association to an object. A theory is abstract, in this sense, if it does not deal with the visible lifeworld; a picture is abstract, in this sense, when no visible object can be discerned in it.

Against the backdrop of these reflections on the concepts "abstract" and "photography" we can understand why it is at least conceivable that the combination of concepts that is "abstract photography" be thought of as a *contradictio in adiecto*. For such is indeed the case if we think the two concepts in their narrow meaning. If by *photography* we understand picturing visible objects by means of cameras, there can be no abstract photography, because this would demand an abstraction from the visible object, the picturing of which, however, is essential to photography in the narrow understanding of the term. This example helps us deduce a fundamental connection between abstraction and photography: it is only possible for us to speak of abstract photography if the concept "photography" denotes for us a phenomenon with contingent properties. We can only abstract from something that which is not considered to be essential to this something. If nothing inessential is present, nothing can be abstracted. It is for this reason that every successful abstraction is also always a reduction to something essential. It follows from the very concept that every abstraction results from an intent to direct attention to those characteristics of a thing that are judged essential. This fundamental connection, precisely, is valid, without restriction, for the particular case of abstraction in photography. Like all abstractions, abstraction in photography must be a reduction to essential aspects, that is, in this case, a reduction to the essential characteristics of photography. For whatever abstract photographs may look like, they too are conceivable *as* abstract photographs—and this is not an empirical but a logical insight—only if they abstract from something that is not essential to photography. If they abstracted from something essential, the result would no longer be a photograph. Someone who understands by photography the technical production of figurative images cannot therefore call nonfigurative photography "photography." This, however, means that abstract photography becomes possible only if the concept "photography" has not already been reduced in such a way that abstraction is no longer possible, that is, only if the concept of photography that is presupposed still maintains a dimension that allows for abstraction.

One understanding of photography that allows for abstraction can be articulated as follows: the concept "photography" denotes processes that produce permanent images by means of optical systems (cameras) and the action of light on substances that react to this effect. If we start with this common understanding, there are two points where a series of questions comes in: Does this definition include inessential characteristics of photography? Is it not possible to forgo one of the listed properties of photography? What of this usual understanding of photography may be left out without our being forced to stop talking about photography? These two points are, first, the process of production (i.e., the taking of photographs) and, second, the product (i.e., the photograph produced); they can be examined as to whether they contain nonessential components.

Abstractions in the process of photographic production

If we start with the production process, the question *What could "abstract photography" be?* is answered by naming the kinds of photography that skip parts of the common process of production. In this respect the part of photographic production that is most often discussed and judged to be "superfluous" is without a doubt the lens, even the camera as a whole. We can think of abstract photography as photography that tries, without complete cameras, to preserve as visible traces the action of light on substances sensitive to light. These purely formal reflections on the concept of abstract photography coincide—could it be otherwise?—with the history of this kind of photography. Indeed, we call abstract photography those areas of experimental photography that try to produce photographs by means of a reduced process of production. The classic examples of abstract photography especially work deliberately without cameras or parts of cameras: Alvin Langdon Coburn's *Vortographs* (fig. 1), Christian Schad's *Shadographies*, Man Ray's *Rayograms*, Gottfried Jäger's *Pinhole Structures* (fig. 2). All of these examples—no matter what they look like—are examples of abstract photography merely by virtue of their abstracting from components of the taking of photographs. We could even say that to a considerable extent the history of abstract photography appears as constantly working on the question *And what else can we do without in the production of a photo?* There are answers of different degrees of radicality: while the *cliché verre* does without a camera, it does not do without a kind of negative. In this technique a glass plate is covered with soot or a similarly opaque layer; then, as in drypoint, a sketch is scratched onto it. Afterward, this glass plate serves as a kind of negative for photographic copying and enlargement processes. The *cliché verre* thus abstracts from the camera but not from the negative—which suggests the next step of abstraction: the *photogram*. The photogram additionally abstracts from the detour via the negative. Objects are placed directly on the photographic paper and influence the light falling onto it, leaving traces to be developed. Yet even this can be escalated: the so-called *luminogram* abstracts not only from the camera and the negative but also from the "pictured object" [*Abbildungsgegenstand*] of the *photogram*. In the case of the luminogram directed and manipulated light shines directly onto the photosensitive paper, without detours through or transformations by a lens, without reflections or shadows from an object.

When we look at this series of conceivable abstractions, we notice that there is an immanent hierarchy inscribed into the techniques of cameraless photography: from the abstraction from the lens, via that from the camera as a whole, from the negative, from the object influencing the path of the light, to the most radical form of abstract photography, which clearly approaches the limits of no-longer-photography: the *chemigram*. Here, it is exclusively combinations of chemicals on photosensitive paper, for example of developer and fixer, that lead to the development of

FIGURE 1.   Alvin Langdon Coburn (USA 1882–1966 GB): *Vortograph*, 1917. New gelatin silver print, 30.6 x 25.5 cm, ca. 1960. L. Fritz Gruber Collection, Museum Ludwig, Cologne. © George-Eastman-House, Rochester, NY.

visible forms under normal light conditions. The chemigram practices a technique that raises the question whether it does not abstract from an essential characteristic of photography, namely from designing and forming the light shining onto the paper. Gottfried Jäger, in any case, does not want to do without this characteristic in a definition of photography: "It is

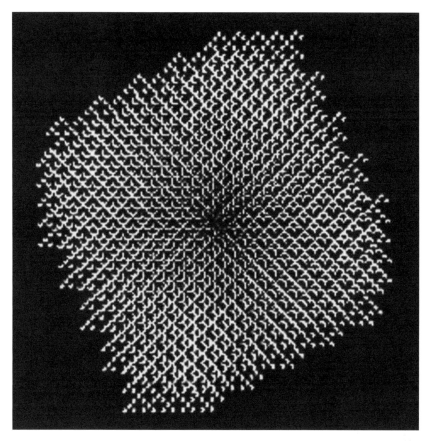

FIGURE 2.   Gottfried Jäger (D 1937): *Lochblendenstruktur* (Pinhole Structures) 3.8.14 F 2.6, 1967. Light graphic. Gelatin silver print, 50 x 50 cm. Collection of the artist. © VG Bild-Kunst, Bonn / Prof. Gottfried Jäger, Bielefeld.

the principle of the analogy between the cause and the effect of the light. Photos are brought about by electromagnetic radiation being channeled and fixed on a material sensitive to radiation. This proposition applies for simple camera photographs, as well as for the most abstract light compositions. Both are the direct result of a physical interplay of causes and effects that they picture each in their own way."[3] Here we see once again that the answer to the question *What could "abstract photography" be?* always depends on one's opinion about what photography is as such. If photographs indeed "are brought about by electromagnetic radiation being channeled," as we just saw, then the chemigram either crosses the boundary of what can be abstracted or it constitutes an extreme kind of interpretation of this characteristic. In this particular case the decision is particularly difficult to make, for the chemicals themselves do indeed sit on the photo paper like an object and act as a light-absorbent and thus light-channeling medium, as is the case for the objects used in the photogram. Yet if this rest of channeling of light were to be essential to a chemigram, we would not be dealing with an autonomous form of abstract photography, just with a variant of the photogram. Yet photograms and chemigrams can very well be distinguished conceptually: the techniques of the photogram influence the path of light from the source onto the light-sensitive material, whereas the techniques of the chemigram influence the effects of light on the light-sensitive material. In the case of the chemigram a photo is thus produced because electromagnetic radiation is channeled and formed in its effect by the photographer. Here, as in the case of every photo, we have the fixed trace of a controlled cooperation of light and light-sensitive material. This is exactly what we should not overlook: in the case of the chemigram we precisely have not abstracted from an essential component of taking photographs, namely from the fixation of a trace of light. It is very well possible to think of dispensing with this fixation, as is the case for so-called *flux* or *fluid images*. Differently disposed light-sensitive substances are exposed to nonformed light and left to this process; what we get is a continuously developing, nonstopped chemigram. Where the light shows what kind of effect might well have been influenced, yet if we demand—as we have just said—that in a photo, channeled radiation is "fixed on a material sensitive to radiation," we have to say that this fixation is missing. Though flow images are conceivable and indeed familiar from Sigmar Polke's work for the 1986 Venice Biennale, they do not fall under the concept of abstract photography because they are no longer photographs at all. In this extreme form of abstraction the photograph is reduced to the mere sequence of a chemical process and is thus dissolved in a conceptual, albeit not a chemical sense.

If we are to judge cameraless photography to be a form of abstract photography, we are well advised to state precisely why this is to be the case. We can think of two reasons. First, we could say that cameraless photography is abstract because it abstracts, during the taking of photographs, from the use of important components of the common process of taking photographs. In this case cameraless photography necessarily leads to results that can be addressed as abstract photography. According to this understanding, if we know that a photo was produced without a camera, we know that the photo must be abstract even without having seen it. This result is more than unsatisfactory, for if we speak of abstract photography, we should also address characteristics of its products. That is why, second, we can be of the opinion that cameraless photography leads to abstract photography because there are no figurative images of objects discernible in its products. Yet this second reason is distinct from the first in that it is no longer possible to sustain the thesis that cameraless photography always and in every case leads to abstract photography. In many photograms we can clearly and distinctly discern objects; the results are not abstract. The *cliché verre* is a photo-supported graphical technique that, like every etching, allows for figurative photographs of objects. Gottfried Jäger's *Pinhole Structures* are produced by an apparatus that, in terms of its principles of construction, is similar to the traditional *camera obscura* and thus could have produced figurative images as well. In short, if we want to consider not only the process of production but also the works, the concepts "cameraless photography" and "abstract photography" can by no means simply be equated. Photography *without* a camera in most cases, yet not necessarily, leads to photographs we call abstract because they do not display an object. And conversely we must make note of the possibility of producing abstract photographs *with* a camera. Therefore, we must conclude that from the perspective of phenomenology and work aesthetics, the process of production is negligible; rather, as announced, the products of abstract photography must be examined as to what about them is contingent and thus capable of being abstracted from.

Abstractions in the photographic product

In the case of an abstract photo it is relatively easy to say what it is *not*: it is not a figurative picture. An abstract photograph is a thing, in most cases a piece of paper, which was produced phototechnically and on which there are visible forms. These forms, in turn, can also be perceived by the viewer as an image object, an image object, however, that either bears only very vague and modest visible resemblance to real objects or none at all. The abstract photo delivers no image object that—as is the case in the so-called figurative picture—could be referred by means of its resemblance to an existent or a fictitious object. Yet how does this negative description help? Saying what an abstract photo is not does not answer the question *What could abstract photographs be?* The problem of abstract photography, remarkably, is not the simple statement that it does not display a recognizable object, but the giving of reasons why and what for an abstract photo abstracts from the depiction of a familiar object. The solution to this problem is related to the phenomenon, already presented above, that every abstraction happens in order to direct attention to something that is judged to be essential. When we abstract, we disregard something and thereby show that we think we can disregard it. Thereby, in turn, we show that what we disregard, from our point of view, cannot be essential, since essential things can, in principle, not be disregarded. That is why every abstraction always leads to an exhibition of what is deemed essential; every abstracting turn away is linked to a visualizing turn toward. This, however, means that abstract photography is only conceivable if its works forgo picturing discernible objects in order to make something else all the more clearly discernible. In the end the question *What could "abstract photography" be?* is not answered by saying that it is nonfigurative photography. This nondisplay can only be a necessary but not a sufficient characteristic of abstract photography since photographs are conceivable that do not display any object and yet are not abstract photographs. On wrapping paper that is produced with photographic means we might see pretty shapes but not discern objects, yet the wrapping paper is not abstract photography since this paper does not forgo displaying something for the sake of something else. Or let us imagine we developed and enlarged the unusable beginning of a common film negative that has accidentally been exposed to light: we would not get an abstract photo. We even have to go so far as to say that nondisplay cannot be the concern proper of abstract photography but only a way of doing something else; if this something else—whatever it is—is not actualized, nonfigurative photography is not abstract photography. The question that stood at the beginning, *What could "abstract photography" be?*, has to be translated more precisely: *What could be reasons for producing photographs in which we cannot discern objects?* Several answers are conceivable; what follows is a presentation of three of them.

Abstraction for the sake of structures of visibility

One answer to the question *What could be reasons for producing photographs in which we cannot discern objects?* that immediately presents itself is the following: these photographs are meant to demonstrate that with the medium of photography we can refer to something other than just objects and that this happens in figurative images as well. If abstract photography abstracts from picturing things for this reason, it is an emphatic self-reflection in the medium of photography. With the means provided by photography, abstract photography wants to answer the question of what a photo is, and to this end it produces photographs that display what in figurative images is an essential, albeit restricted, not independent, part. This part is the "how" of the photo, the formal structures of a photograph that make it possible for a figurative photograph to do what it does, namely display an object. Every photograph comes about by means of light traces being developed into visible forms on a piece of paper. Yet these visible forms, their figures and internal relations, serve a purpose: they exist not for their own sake but to allow something to become visible, to display what they themselves are not. When we look at a figurative picture, we would not say we were looking at forms and colors. Even though the forms are what we see, our gaze, our intentional attention, is directed toward the image object. Yet this image object is only visible because there are forms and colors, even though these do not as such enter the gaze of the normal viewer. This does not, however, mean that they could not be made visible. This is one reason for abstraction: the abstract picture can forgo displaying a thing in order thus to show how a photo displays an object. Looking at the image object demands that we overlook the infrastructure. That is why an abstract photo could be a photo that tries to display the otherwise overlooked structures themselves. Something overlooked is being thematized. If an abstract picture forgoes displaying a thing for this reason, the forms and colors in the abstract photo are something fundamentally different from the forms and colors on a wallpaper: they are the forms and colors that this medium can also use for the depiction of objects. Every photo—that is, the figurative photo, too—comes about in a process of structure formation. And precisely because this is the case for objective photographs as well, abstraction from the objectivity of photographs is a reduction of the picture to the very aspect that is essential to photography as a whole, essential because no kind of photography can forgo it: we cannot create a photo that does not develop visible structures. The structures and forms we see in abstract photography, according to this understanding, are the structures and forms that could display something but display nothing. We could also say that the abstract photo presents itself as a potential figurative photo, for it relates to the figurative picture the way an incomplete part relates to the whole. This interpretation applies not only to abstract photographs but, from the point of view of phenomenology at least, to abstract images in general. Roman Ingarden, for one, explicitly underlines this point: "I merely want to call attention to the fact that a, so to speak, non-representational picture enters into the structure of every presentational picture as an indispensable component of it."[4] In every figurative picture there are structures that are liberated in the abstract picture. This means that the abstract photo is a kind of experiment for the question *What makes a photograph possible?* The procedures, already mentioned, of reducing the conventional process of production accord well with this quasi-media theoretical self-understanding; so, too, however, does abstract camera photography that radically concentrates on macro and micro structures (as does, for example, the work of Carl Strüwe [fig. 3]). In this last case the structures of photography are almost literally put under the microscope by means of photography; what happens, therefore, is what, metaphorically, is the concern of abstract photography as a whole, namely the isolation and emancipation of photographic surface structures. Yet this also means, and this is decisive, that the structures in an abstract picture thus understood cannot be merely ornamental forms because they do indeed have meaning: even though they do not refer to objects, they yet can be used to refer to the structure of other possible photographs that display objects. Seen this way, abstract photography is, as Gottfried Jäger aptly puts it, a "photography of photography": "In it, the photo process is broken down into its elements, components and structures. . . . No longer the 'what' or the 'who' are at the focus of interest but the 'how.'"[5]

Abstraction for the sake of visibility

A second answer to the question *What could be reasons for producing photographs on which we cannot discern objects?*, an answer that does

FIGURE 3. Carl Strüwe (D 1898–1988): *Ein Kristall ist geboren* (A Crystal Was Born), 1946. Microphotograph. Crystals of asparagine acid. Gelatin silver vintage print, 54.7 x 43.8 cm. Kunsthalle Bielefeld. © VG Bild-Kunst, Bonn/Prof. Gottfried Jäger, Bielefeld.

not present itself as immediately as the first, is the following: these photographs are meant to show that photographs can be images that do not have to refer to anything at all. This thesis can be formulated differently: abstract photography is meant to show that photographs can be images that are not signs. Everything that is used for referring is a sign, and in the first answer the structures indeed are used to refer to something: they exemplify the possibilities of photographic picturing [*Abbilden*]. The structural formations in an abstract photograph in the first answer are used as signs: they stand for how something can become visible in a photo. Yet does it have to be this way? We could think of an escalation: does the turn away from the object have to be a turn toward the "how" of photographic displaying? It can be; that is not the question. But can the turn away from the object not also be linked to a turn to something other than the "how" of displaying? This question concerns the sign character of abstract photography. It is easily conceivable that an abstract photo also fulfill semiotic purposes. This is not surprising, if only because every object and thus also every image can be used as a sign. Yet, once more, the opposite, too, is at least conceivable, namely that an abstract photo forgoes displaying a familiar image object in order to consciously create an image object that is not to be used as a sign at all. What is to be created is, as it were, an image object that refuses the obvious use as a sign for a thing that bears visible resemblance to it because this image object does not, at least not in this way, bear resemblance to any known real thing.

In the case of a figurative image we construct an object whose visibility we are familiar with, for example an exclusively visible house. In the abstract photo, however, we are concerned with constructing objects from pure visibility, objects that bear no resemblance to real things but are simply new, visibly determined objects, just as we are capable of constructing both familiar and new objects outside of images. If we understand abstract photography in this sense, then the medium of photography is not used for picturing [*abbilden*] or visibly reproducing something but for forming [*bilden*] and visibly producing something. The medium becomes a tool for the generation of an artificial object. The concept of generative photography aptly captures this understanding of the sense and purpose of abstract photography: "It's not giving reality to a concept, it's presenting a reality—that's photography."[6] Yet we have to be careful: the concepts "generative photography" and "abstract photography" are not identical: abstract photography can be generative, but it does not have to be, as the first answer has shown. The first form was unambiguously nonfigurative; it was concerned with the infrastructure of the image. Yet the generative form of abstract photography is itself figurative—not in the sense that it pictures an object but in the sense that it generates an actual object, albeit a nonphysical object with the sole property of being visible. The image object is understood as an abstract sculpture but not because a real abstract sculpture has been photographed; by means of the photographic medium new, concrete, albeit exclusively visible, sculptures are created. Hence generative photography relates to abstract photography the way an incomplete part relates to the whole, and this is why generative photography can also be called concrete photography: something concrete is created. It is important to note, though, that what is meant, of course, is not the photo paper as a concrete object in the normal sense of the term but the object visible on the paper. *Luminograms*, as they were produced, for example, in the 1950s by Peter Keetman (fig. 4), make this kind of abstract photography graspable. All we have to ask when we turn to this kind of photography is, *What do we see in them?* We see an object whose precise, usually intricate, appearance we may well be able to describe precisely yet an object that has nothing but just such an exclusively visible appearance. Pure visibility has become the only thing present; we are dealing with a new object of pure visibility that bears no resemblance to an existing real object and cannot even be thought as a real object. Since we have not previously known an object that looked like this, we have created, by means of a photograph and in a sense as simple as it is fundamental, a new object sui generis. Put more effusively: in abstract photography, the world grows richer not in semblance [*Schein*] but in being [*Sein*].

Abstraction for the sake of object art

A third answer to the question *What could be reasons for producing photographs on which we cannot discern objects?* is the following: these photographs are meant to show that photographs do not have to be images at all. This answer might be shocking, for it abstracts from something widely regarded to be self-evident, namely that photographs are always images.

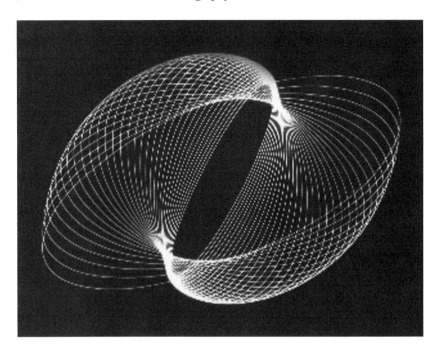

FIGURE 4.   Peter Keetman (D 1916–2005): *Schwingungsfigur 995* (Light Pendulum Figure 995), 1951. Camera luminogram. Gelatin silver vintage print, 17.4 x 23.4 cm. Gottfried Jäger Collection, Bielefeld © Stiftung F. C. Gundlach Foundation, Hamburg.

That this is almost always the case is beyond doubt; almost everything that is produced photographically is an image. Yet here, too, the decisive question can only be *Does it have to be this way, or can we also think of it differently?* Could it not be that the use of photography for the production of images is a contingent—albeit widespread—use? Could we not think of photographs that are not images? We have here a question that targets the center of abstract photography. Abstract photography makes it its program to produce photographs that abstract from the contingent properties of the medium in order to emphasize its noncontingent properties; thus, it must of course ask itself if not perhaps the pictorial character as a whole is contingent for photography. Alvin Langdon Coburn, fitting for a first ancestor, may have been the first to suspect this, since he titled his 1916 programmatic essay on abstract photography *The Future of Pictorial Pho-*

tography. Coburn's title suggests that his concern is a photography that is to be pictorial and precisely not nonpictorial. Yet if nothing else were conceivable, then Coburn would not have had to speak explicitly of "pictorial photography"; then the concept "pictorial photography" (which, by the way, appears frequently in current debates) would be a pleonasm. But it is precisely not logically necessary that the products of abstract photography be pictures, or even images. Coburn thus suggests that he is concerned with a certain kind of abstract photography. We could also approach the problem raised here from another angle: what is the next highest genus to the concept "abstract photography"? There are two equally conceivable candidates, "abstract image" and "abstract art." Is the meaning of the concept "abstract photography" contained in the meaning of the concept "abstract image" or in the meaning of the concept "abstract art," or in equal parts in both? If abstract photography understands itself to be a part of abstract art, then we do indeed have to pay attention to the fact that not every image is a work of art and that, conversely, not every work of art is an image. In consequence it is very well conceivable that abstract photography in its abstraction could strive for the production of objects that are photographs but not images. The turn away from the depiction of an object in a photograph thus can also be understood so radically as to lead to a turn away generally from the production of images. In this case the techniques of photography are employed not in order to produce images but to produce things, objects, or parts of installations—yet this in turn is done with the intention of pointing at a possibility that photography offers. In this sense it is conceivable that the place of pictorial [*bildmäßig*] photography be filled by an artistic [*kunstmäßig*] photography. Given the development of art in the twentieth century, this step very much seems to suggest itself, for artists examine photography not only as to how to create artistic images but also as to how to create nonpictorial art. Twentieth-century art is to a large extent characterized by the discovery that technically produced objects can have the status of art. What in object art is deemed art is not an image but precisely a concrete object. We are here dealing with works of art that are not images. Abstract photography, then, is a contribution to object art when it uses photography not for the production of images but precisely for that of objects. These works of abstract photography still fit the concept of generative and concrete photography.

FIGURE 5.   Gottfried Jäger (D 1937): *Graukeil* (Grayscale), 1983. Photo object. Unique gelatin silver paper, 25 x 25 cm. Collection of the artist © 2007 by VG Bild-Kunst, Bonn / Prof. Gottfried Jäger, Bielefeld.

Yet we must also see that the concept here acquires a meaning different from the one we outlined above. For now it is no longer the production of a concrete object in the image, that is, the generation of a thing from pure visibility, we are dealing with; it is the production of a thing that, like any normal thing, can be touched and smelt. The examples for such an understanding of abstract photography are numerous, but one must suffice: Gottfried Jäger's 1983 *Graukeil* [Gray Card] (fig. 5). In this work no picturing [*Abbilden*] of anything takes place; it is not about the pictorial production of a purely pictorial visibility but exclusively about the use of the photograph in the material sense as part of an installation. In *Graukeil* the photo paper, which in objective photography usually displays three-dimensional things, becomes three-dimensional itself: the material that displays takes the place of what is pictorially displayed. The photo paper as a real object ousts the imaginary image object—and thus ousts the image from a work of art.

What could "abstract photography" be?

Answering the question *What could "abstract photography" be?* leads to at least three possible conceptions. It is possible to forgo displaying a thing through photography, first, for the sake of image-immanent structures; second, for the sake of mere visibility; and, third, for the sake of object art. Whatever the history and reality of abstract photography may look like, it cannot but conform to the possibilities—but it does so unambiguously only in the rarest of cases. What can and should be clearly separated conceptually is in reality most of the time indissolubly blended, and it is not rare for such blending to constitute the appeal of a thing. This is particularly true for works of art that very often cannot easily be categorized, that refuse to be categorized, or that fit several categories at once. Yet—and this really is decisive—this recalcitrance of reality toward clear typologies does not testify against the necessity clearly to separate conceptually fundamental possible conceptions—it merely speaks for art.

5

Windows, TVs, and Windows Again

Hardly any metaphor has marked the reflection on images—and on media as a whole—as much as Leon Batista Alberti's famous comparison of the image to an open window in *De Pictura*. Alberti finished his treatise in 1435, after which it circulated in manuscript copies, not to be printed until 1540. A few sentences by this Renaissance artist and theoretician suffice to sketch an image of the image that is as intelligible as it is convincing: "First I draw on the surface to be painted a quadrangle of right angles, of any size, that for me is an open window [*aperta finestra*] through which the 'process' [*istoria*] is being looked at."[1] All reservations that have been voiced against this comparison notwithstanding, in one central point we must agree with Alberti: the material image on the wall is like a window because in both cases the viewer looks through a transparent plane without thematizing the transparent plane itself. The look we take at the image, as well as the look we take through the window, directs our attention toward things and events that are not in the same space. By means of a window, we normally look out of a house at the outside; by means of an image, we see an image object in an imaginary space. Images and windows make it possible to look at something other than themselves.

It is this self-denial of the medium that phenomenological image theories thematize and describe more precisely under the heading "transparency of the image." Hence it is not surprising that Jean-Paul Sartre, for example, in his phenomenological philosophy of the image explicitly works with Alberti's metaphor: "If the painter," he writes in "What Is Literature?," "presents us with a field or a vase of flowers, his paintings are windows that open onto the whole world."[2] Yet Edmund Husserl, too, uses the window metaphor: "We look through the frame, as if through a window, into the space of the image."[3] At first Husserl seems to be of one opinion with Alberti: "In the case of a perfect portrait that perfectly presents the person with respect to all of his moments (all that can possibly be distinctive), indeed, even in a portrait that does this in a most unsatisfactory way, it feels to us as if the person were there himself."[4]

Yet it is with this very thesis that we capture the problem connected, in the philosophy of the image, with the metaphor of the open window. For it simply cannot be said, as this metaphor claims, that the viewer of a photo feels "as if the person were there himself." There is an obvious difference in the mode of givenness: when we see a person through a window, this seeing is always linked to a consciousness of the real presence of what is seen. We look out of the window into an existing world; yet this is in no way the case for looking at an image. Husserl describes this difference in a particularly precise way by the concept of a conflict, and he is thus able to determine the limits of Alberti's metaphor of the open window. The comparison to the window does not do justice to the conflictual mode of givenness of an image object. A thing depicted in an image "appears," Husserl writes, "in the way in which an actual physical thing appears, but in conflict with the actual presence [*Gegenwart*] that conflict-free perception brings about."[5] This means that looking at the image does not lead us to feel "as if the person were there himself" at all. Our practical dealings with images confirm this description: hardly anyone will look at an image and then greet the person depicted there because he or she presumes that person to be present. Hardly any of us call the police when we see a murder on TV. The appearance of a thing in the image does not possess the unbroken character of the immediate presence of that thing, which presence is characteristic of the view through a window: "The appearance [*Erscheinung*] still has a characteristic that prevents us from taking it as the appearance of something itself [*Selbsterscheinung*] in the strictest sense."[6] That is why, from a phenomenological point of view, the common image can precisely not be treated like a window.

If the phenomenological descriptions are accurate, then the television set [*Fernseher*],[7] at first sight, seems to be a relapse into Alberti's prephenomenological time—that is, not the television set itself but the claim articulated in its name. For the name *television* suggests that the apparatus of this name possesses the capacity to afford a view into the distance. Indeed, both the name *television* and the inventions that were decisive for its developments originate from the effort to construct a telephone for the eyes. The first use of the term *television* [*Fernsehen*] in print can be found in Raphael Eduard Liesegang's 1891 *Beiträge zum Problem des electrischen Fernsehens* [Contributions on the Problem of Electrical Television]. Liesegang makes it perfectly clear that the function of the television set is not to bring about the telegraphy of images; rather, it is concerned with electrical seeing at a distance. This at least can be glimpsed from the headline "Distant Electric Vision," under which the *London Times* reports on current developments toward television in 1911. We can see that the name *television* [*Fernseher*] is a radicalization of Alberti's metaphor, for the name compares television [*Fernsehen*] in the living room not only to the view from a lookout point into the distance but first and foremost to looking through a telescope. The tele-scope is the classical instrument of tele-vision. With a good telescope, we see out of the window even better: further into the distance, more clearly, even at twilight. And it is this capacity of the telescope that the television is to improve further electronically: in 1884 Paul Nipkow, who is often referred to as the inventor of the television set, has his idea patented as—in his formulation—an "electrical telescope." The famous first sentence of this patent reads: "The apparatus to be described here has the purpose of making an object in location *A* visible at any other location *B*."[8] This makes it clear that the name *television* for the TV set stands in the tradition of the open window that makes a good view into the distance possible. The invention of the TV is the actualization of windows that are even better than those we are familiar with from normal houses. It is the actualization of literally fabulous windows. Or so we may say, given that we can find a description of these perfect tele-vision-windows, a description that is as early as it is precise, in the opening sentences of the fairy tale *The Sea-Hare*, published in 1857 by the Grimm brothers:

There was once upon a time a Princess, who, high under the battlements in her castle, had an apartment with twelve windows, which looked out in every possible direction, and when she climbed up to it and looked around her, she could inspect her whole kingdom. When she looked out of the first, her sight was more keen than that of any other human being; from the second she could see still better, from the third more distinctly still, and so it went on, until the twelfth, from which she saw everything above the earth and under the earth, and nothing at all could be kept secret from her.[9]

In short, the invention of television actualizes a fabulous window—and this is exactly how TV manufacturers pitch their apparatus as late as the 1950s: "You really have the beautiful illusion that the screen of your receiver is a kind of window, an additional window in your home—a window that opens for you a view into the world."[10]

The only question is whether the claim articulated in the name *television* is justified, or whether the name is not merely a name. Just because TVs have been designated "televisions," this does not mean that the properties expressed in the name really are present. Kurt Schwitters would say: Greenwich Village is no village either.[11] In the absence of further reasons we thus must not conclude from its name anything about the claims, properties, and capacities of a thing. The TV set, one obvious criticism of its name could go, simply does not do justice to its name, because in reality it is nothing more than just another medium for moving images [*Laufbilder*], and images, as we saw earlier with Husserl as well, are not windows, never mind telescopes, but simply depictions. As convincing as this objection may be at first sight, we still have to ask how such a misnomer of the television set could come about; we can, after all, explain why Greenwich Village is not called Greenwich Neighborhood.

The denomination of the television set is only appropriate if we presume that the name refers exclusively to the possibilities newly created by this medium: the TV set—completely in accordance with Nipkow's intention—is not primarily a medium of storage but a medium of transmission. It is possible to watch movies on TV, but that is not a specific capacity of the TV; we can do that in the movie theater as well. When we watch a movie on TV, we use the TV not as television but as home cinema, as a movie theater substitute. Only when we watch live transmissions do we use the TV as television, for in that case we let ourselves be shown something that only television can show, something that is not a film but a broadcast. By the standard of the specific capacity of television technology for live transmissions, the denomination is extraordinarily appropriate. For in live reporting we are indeed presented with a present, that is, a simultaneous event in the distance. When it functions this way, the television replaces a conceivable telescope. For the viewer knows very well how to distinguish a car crash in a film from the live broadcast of a Formula One race. In this latter case the viewer watches a real event in the distance, which unfolds in the very moment of viewing but withdraws from direct view. This shows us what series the TV forms part of: we can watch an actual Formula One race from the stands, from the window of an adjacent building, through a telescope from an adjoining hill, or by means of a live broadcast on television. When we place the TV in this series and also recall Alberti's metaphor of the window, the invention of the television constitutes a particularly idiosyncratic situation. We have here a medium that is better than the view from the window or through any telescope. From what window, after all, can we watch all Formula One races in the world? With television we have a medium that allows us to see simultaneous but removed events in many places. Yet we do not have images that display something present in the vicinity of the viewer. The artificial presence of an event in a live broadcast only concerns its simultaneous visibility. We use the TV to see a present, that is to say, a momentary event in the distance, but we hardly watch it as if we saw a present race within our own four walls. We precisely do not see a race that takes place in the living room, but we see, in the living room, a race that takes place at the same time in a country far away. Everything we see on television is in the distance. From the point of view of media history, the invention of an apparatus for the tele-vision of this race in the living room imposes the task of inventing an apparatus for its peri-vision. We could also say that we still need a medium that really lives up to Alberti's window comparison, a medium by means of which we see something that is close. Television provides us with an apparatus that may replace fabulous windows and telescopes but does not replace the normal shop window [*Schaufenster*].[12] For in this latter we see real things in a display up close. This possibility belongs to the properties of all windows: through a window we also see things that are present in the sense of "closely present"—things that someone looking through the window might well interact with. For example, we may greet someone through a window, throw the keys down through an open window, or buy the things presented in the shop window. In the case of the shop window we do not look from out of a room into the distance but into a space that is close. This is a generally valid point: the things up close that are visible through a window belong within the radius of things that can be interacted with—and this is something television cannot offer because it displays things that, as its name indicates, are distant. It removes everything into the distance. This is a medial property: no matter what television lets us see, close as it may be, it is distanced by the television. Everything the TV lets us see, it displays as if it just took place in the distance—and this is precisely something we often appreciate: television delivers, right into our homes, something required for a feeling of sublimity, namely, that what is seen is at a safe distance.

Microsoft's *Windows* is probably the computer operating system most commonly used. It resembles the older Apple *Mac OS* like an identical twin. Yet in one point the knockoff is extraordinarily inventive: in its choice of name, *Windows*. The name refers to the idea that the user of the system sees what he or she wants to see on the screen always within an available area that is called, precisely, a window. As the art historian Axel Müller has pointed out, the presence of Alberti's metaphor is on display here.[13] Hence it is appropriate to ask to what extent what Alberti meant with his metaphor actualizes itself here. Such actualization would precisely be the case if, like shop windows, the windows on the screen were to let us see things that are in attendance.

Imagine a situation in which someone uses a computer that runs Windows for text processing; he or she writes a text into the area that is called a window. This text, which can then be read in the screen window, is a text that is present and that the viewer has access to, that he or she can modify the way he or she could modify a text written with pencil on a piece of paper. In such a window the viewer of a computer screen is not afforded a view onto an absent text; rather, by means of an image a text has been produced that is visible and in attendance. This is the function of the screen window: that of a pictorial medium for producing and presenting things that are in attendance. A screen is a display for the presentation of things—yet not for the presentation of real things but rather for that of virtual things. Its windows, in this sense, are actual windows (like shop windows) through which we look into a space filled with artificially present things. These are always different from the things we could see through the windows of houses; they are visible-only, nonphysical things that can only be produced by means of images. Hence we can say that in this case the image becomes identical to a window. This identity is particularly clear if we think of a window containing the simulation of an event, for example the simulation of a Formula One race. In that case we would have the inversion of television, indeed a perivision that brings a virtual race into the living room. The television becomes a monitor, of which Herbert W. Franke aptly writes: "The screen forms a kind of window that makes the view into an unlimited space possible."[14] This artificial window is not one we look through into the distance but, as through a shop window, into what Husserl said above was an "image space." This space is not unlimited in the sense of being infinitely large. Rather, in it new things are visible, without limits—without limits because they become freely available and manipulable: "The parts of the image that are not visible at the moment can be stored or—an interesting possibility—they can be generated by the program only when the viewer approaches a particular edge of the image."[15] In concrete terms, if we look at the simulation of a race on the monitor, we do not look at a simultaneous race in the distance by means of a telescope substitute, but we look at a virtual race that takes place in an immediate vicinity, we could say, in an observable space neighboring the viewer's. That is why the windows on a computer screen are both images and windows: windows because they give us something to be seen that we can interact with through the window, images because they give us something to see that is not really but only artificially present, that is, something exclusively visible. No doubt this is not a phenomenon Alberti could have thought of, but this does not preclude the fact that every time we open a computer window, we put Alberti's theory of the image as an open window into practice in an unthought-of way: through a window [*Schaufenster*] a view opens into an imaginary image space filled with nonphysical things.

Virtual Reality: The Assimilation of the Image to the Imagination

Virtual reality and immersion

Sometimes we can understand a line of argument particularly well when we know what someone does *not* want to say. In the case at hand we are concerned with a criticism of the thought that virtual realities emerge from a perfect assimilation of images to perception—an idea that is common in current image theory. When we take a look at the definitive publications on the history of virtual reality, at least, we quickly find numerous examples that equate virtual reality with the phenomenon of so-called immersive images. The thesis is, "Virtual realities—both past and present—are in essence immersive."[1] What is understood by immersive image is that kind of image that has the viewer believe that the thing displayed in the image is actually present. Work in virtual reality accordingly pursues the goal of "producing a high-grade feeling . . . of presence,"[2] which in the extreme case is so strong that the viewer of the image regards the thing that is visible, artificially present, as a real thing, even confuses one with the other. The viewer thus dives into the depicted image world and believes him- or herself to be at the place of depiction; hence also the theological concept of immersion, which literally denotes submersion during baptism.

Western art knows many attempts at the creation of immersive images. The great milestones have become famous; first place has to go to the great panoramas of the nineteenth century. By means of a specific combination of architecture with an all-around image, the panorama attempts to construct a frameless image without iconic difference from its surroundings. The programmatic goal is the actualization of a panoramic view, as if one saw the thing—in most instances a city—itself. Or think of the stereoscope, where glasses bring two single images to the eyes; this produces a cunningly real three-dimensional impression of what is displayed. Modern, computer-controlled cyberspace stands in this tradition. Here, too, the image viewer is wearing glasses—the so-called head-mounted display. No movement of the head will lead the viewer's gaze beyond a frame out of the image. In the ideal case, at least, we are dealing with an unrecognizable simulation of perception, a perfect 360-degree simulation. The visitor of a cyberspace might still know but no longer perceives that he or she is in a virtual reality. This technology perfects immersion; the perception of a depiction has been assimilated indistinguishably to the perception of the real world—yet this is not the problem. Even if cyberspace technology were to become widespread, it is not the relevant and dominant phenomenon currently addressed as virtual reality. The following objection, rather, seems justified: if we equate virtual reality with the phenomenon of immersive images, we take as our guide an undoubtedly quite extreme and rare form of images. We can therefore not explain why the common use of the phrase *virtual realities* refers to distinctly recognizable images as well—and this precisely is normally the case—for it is not, by any means, common usage to mean by virtual realities, or by virtual objects, the phenomenon of immersion, the matrix, or a cyberspace. On the contrary, mostly, we speak of virtual realities in the case of images that do not stand in the tradition of the panorama or the stereoscope in any way whatsoever. Think of a simulation on a computer screen or of a normal video game: it is quite typical to speak of a virtual reality in these cases, even though these images on screens are not immersive. No viewer mistakes an image object on a computer screen with reality. Because of the conflicting frame, the iconic difference, and the stylistic ways of seeing, every image on a screen is clearly a nonimmersive image—and yet we commonly speak, in the case of video games on TV screens, of virtual realities. For this reason alone it hardly makes sense any longer to address the idea of the immersive image by the concept of virtual reality. The rather rare phenomenon of immersion is not of essential significance to a virtual reality; a virtual reality may very well be immersive, but it does not at all have to be such. We must, rather, distinguish two different variations of virtual reality: immersive virtual reality (as we know it from cyberspace) and nonimmersive virtual reality (as we know it from video games). It is remarkable that immersive virtual reality indeed emerges from the assimilation of the perception of the image object to the perception of a real thing, but nonimmersive virtual reality emerges from an assimilation of the image object to the imagination. This assimilation to objects in the imagination is what is new about the images produced by the new media.

One's opinion on whether the new media have produced images of a new kind is highly dependent on one's understanding of virtual reality. As art historians rightly emphasize, the idea of immersion is very old; it is not born with the new media, which at the most serve better to actualize it. That is why immersion hardly helps in drawing a strong distinction between the images of traditional media and the images of digital media. We must therefore ask whether the new media have merely led to an easy accessibility and a mass proliferation of images and, perhaps, to an improvement of immersion effects, or whether, beyond this, images of a new kind have emerged. If the latter is the case, the term *new media* should not be capitalized, for we have a concept justified by its object. If the newness, however, is not precisely determinable, capitalization is appropriate, for the supposed description is a mere name—and a name, as we know, does not necessarily have anything to do with the thing it means. For this reason we can say that the banal fact that the expression "New Media" is capitalized as often as it is not rather appropriately mirrors the state of the debate about the serious conceptual problem connected to this question of orthography. There is a lively discussion under way in image theory about the newness of new media, a debate that opposes two parties. On one side there are the theoreticians of continuity—we could also call them the "apologists of capitalization." They see a continual development without leaps that connects a first century AD wall painting in the Pompeian *Villa dei Misteri* to a computer-generated virtual reality. Virtual reality, accordingly, is not really anything new but simply the perfect application of something long thematized in art; it is the optimization of immersion. We can note for the record that when virtual reality is defined by means of immersion, we are led to a theory of continuation. On the other side we have the theoreticians of discontinuity, those who see the development of digital media as marking the beginning of an age of images of a new kind. In the second half of the twentieth century, digital technologies created the technical preconditions for the production of virtual realities that did not previously exist in such high quality. Phenomenologists in particular, not least among them Vilém Flusser, attempt to describe precisely what is specifically new about the new media and about virtual reality: namely, that in the last four decades digital technologies have allowed for a previously unknown form of the assimilation of the image to the human imagination to play itself out. It is well worth a try to describe this assimilation—and this, precisely, can only be done comparatively.

Perception, imagination, and image consciousness

Images can be studied by means of two kinds of comparisons: external and internal. External comparisons confront the image with phenomena that themselves are not images; the medium of the image is to be understood by comparing it to, for example, conceptual language, instruments of measurement, human perception, cognitive capacities, or even machines. Internal comparisons, in contrast, oppose different types of images; here, beyond the question of their status as art, photographs, paintings, panoramas, animations, comics, films, and other types of images are put in relation with one another in order to study where the medially conditioned possibilities and limits of the image are located. Yet important as it is to always have a secure methodological awareness of this distinction of external and internal comparisons, it is just as tempting and rewarding to link and combine these two kinds of comparison. In this latter case we ask how different types of images relate to an external phenomenon. Such a combination of internal and external comparisons makes sense precisely when we attempt to describe the medially conditioned kind of visibility of these new images.

Compare the following three horses: first, a real horse that is seen on a real pasture; second, a horse that is conceived of in fantasy; and third, a horse that is seen depicted in an image—for example one of the horses in Ferdinand Hodler's great 1909 painting *Auszug deutscher Studenten in den Freiheitskrieg* [Departure of German Students Joining the War of Liberation], which hangs in the auditorium of Jena's Friedrich Schiller University. The three cases compared here have one obvious thing in common: in all three cases a consciousness is intentionally oriented toward a horse. Seeing, conceiving, and looking at an image produce not in the same way, but to the same extent, a consciousness of something. But this general stating of intentionality is too vague. What is missing for a description of each kind of intentionality is the description of the *differentia specifica* with which each of the psychic modes distinguishes itself from the others: "Every consciousness," Sartre writes, "posits its object, but each in its own way."[3] From this follows methodologically that when we see a horse, conceive of it, or look at it in an image, we are, in different ways, conscious of a horse; therefore, it is our task to determine the particular kind of givenness of each of these modes of consciousness.

The kind of givenness is particularly clear for the consciousness of perception. Perceptions always imply a consciousness of a thing's being in attendance [*Anwesenheit*]. Phenomenology since Husserl rightly speaks about perception in terms of "presentation" [*Präsentation*] and "presenting" [*Gegenwärtigung*], for the consciousness of perception is always a consciousness of something that is meant to be really present. Anyone who thinks that he sees a thing also believes that the thing exists and is present. It is unthinkable that what someone believes to see not also appears as present to this someone. The way the imagination is given is completely different: when we imagine something in our fancy, we are conscious of something we do not regard as present (pathological cases aside). The imagination posits its object as a nothing—to cite Sartre's famous characterization of imagination. In this comparison the strength and particularity of the medium of the image immediately becomes strikingly distinct. Looking at images generates a consciousness that mediates between the imagination and perception. Image consciousness shares with perception the intuitiveness [*Anschaulichkeit*] of a concrete thing; the viewer of Hodler's painting believes that he or she sees horses and students in the image. But this is only one side of his or her way of being with horses. For image consciousness shares with the imagination the unreality of the intentional object. The viewer of Hodler's painting precisely does not believe that he sees real horses; the image is not immersive.

The comparison, therefore, shows that the image object stands between the object of perception and the object of the imagination. On the one hand, it possesses properties of perception, for the viewer of an image thinks he or she can see it. Yet on the other hand, the image object has properties of the imagination, for the viewer nonetheless does not think of it as really being in attendance. But, and this is what makes the whole thing so interesting for media theory, this intermediate position of the image object between the objects of perception and the objects of fantasy, a position that can be described phenomenologically by means of external comparison, is by no means the same for each and every image medium—quite the contrary. An internal comparison can show that different image media significantly differ where external comparison is concerned. The newness of the new media consists precisely in the computer's facilitation of the production of images that, first, move away from the intermediate position just described in previously unknown ways and, second, radically assimilate to the mode of givenness of fantasy objects in the way in which they present the viewer with an image object.

Protean transformability

If in fantasy we conceive of a horse, this horse can move; we can have our fantasized horse gallop or jump—just as we please, at least so long as we confine ourselves to conscious fantasies. One of the most important properties of conscious fantasy is that it orients itself toward something that seems arbitrarily changeable, and changeable in a very particular way, a way that Edmund Husserl calls "the protean character of phantasy."[4] The imaginary object of fantasy can suddenly become another object, can be moved and manipulated—and all of this without any hindrance, any friction, any resistance whatsoever. Since Ovid, fantasy has been the realm of perfect metamorphoses. There are no insurmountable obstacles—not reality's annoying rigidity that humans have to struggle with from morning till night. The worlds of fantasy are neither rigid nor soft—physics has no role to play in them. This renders the difference between the protean changeability of the content of fantasy and an image object readily apparent: an object displayed in an image, in principle, is not changeable at all. It is, of course, possible to paint completely new images, but the things displayed in an already existing image cannot be changed. Even if some idiot destroyed Hodler's image, he or she wouldn't be able to make the depicted horses trot. An image displays a dynamic event, but the visible image object itself is frozen in a moment and a situation. This is by no means a weakness of the easel image; on the contrary, it is a strength that is exploited impressively in Western art in particular. Better than any refrigerator, the easel picture can freeze, conserve, and present to both the investigative and the contemplative gaze situations and fleeting states of mind [*Befindlichkeiten*]. This is the difference in principle between the medium of the easel picture and the medium of film.

Film makes the moving image object possible. It would be easy to make a movie in which horses gallop and the students painted by Hodler leave for the war. The comparison of easel painting and film thus clarifies more than the banality that film can display a dynamic intentional image object. The way in which a change in the film gives itself to the viewer is fundamentally different from the protean changeability of free fantasy. There are no guarantees about where fantasies may lead. We start to conceive of something and to elaborate on it, and nobody knows where we will end up. Even if we want to think the same thing twice, we can never be sure in advance that indeed we will. Whatever we conceive of remains susceptible to the influence of the will, at least in an only phenomenal, not a naturalistic, sense: such as it appears in conscious and willful fantasy. Changes in fantasy, in this respect, seem comparable to driving a car. For in that case the driver has to steer constantly in order to drive where he or she wants to go. Even if the driver only has to go straight, he or she does not move, like a passenger in a streetcar, on a fixed track. The structural affinity is clear: even if we conceive of a horse stopped in its movement, the way horses can be seen in a stopped moment in Hodler's image, we must operate this stopping; we must will that the horse is a horse that stands still and continues to stand still. We can say that an aspect, "which is absent in physical pictoriality, discloses itself," namely that "in physical pictoriality, the image in question is usually a stable image. . . . But here in phantasy presentation the image is something fluctuating, unsteady, changing, now growing in fullness and force, now diminishing, hence something continually changing immanently in the scale of perfection."[5] Or, in the vocabulary of the transcendental, the conditions of the possibility of fantasizing do not allow for any fixing [*Feststellen*] without willful fixation [*Feststellung*]. In that sense we are dealing here with a form of intuition, though not with—as in Kant—a form of perception but with a form of fantasy. For it is the design of the faculty of fantasy that compels it to hold on to and control everything fantasized. Fantasy, to be sure, is like a medium but a medium in which the static nature of the fantasized is not a property conditioned by the medium. This means that fantasy might, metaphorically speaking, produce mental images but not mental photographs—and no mental films either. For the kind of movement we find in films corresponds structurally to the movement inside a streetcar: the mode of givenness of a film's dynamics, in this regard, is diametrically opposed to the autonomy and controllability of one's own free fantasy. If we want to see different events depicted in a film, we have to put another cassette into the VCR. Similarly, we have to change trains, but not automobiles, if en route we change our mind about our destination. There is therefore a clear phenomenological difference in the mode of givenness of movements in free conception and cinematic depiction. Yet the determinedness of film's dynamics is no deficiency at all, as might be thought. Like the determinedness of the still image, this determinedness is first of all a medium-specific property that is established by the conceivable possibilities and limits and, beyond that, is frequently interpreted in artistic films as a strength, in particular when film serves as a medium of narration; for with film it is possible to tell a story in which is laid down exactly what is depicted when and for how long. This is why a specific possibility of the medium of film is exploited whenever the inner logic of a story, a story whose events are to appear to the viewer as an inevitable development, is unfolded.[6]

Film and animation

The immense difference in the mode in which changes in the flow of the imaginary and in the flow of cinematic images give themselves becomes an appropriate starting point when we want to turn toward the new forms of moving images we find in digital media. But to say it clearly from the get-go: what is decisive for the newness of the digital images is *not* that they were produced digitally. Mosaics have always had a digital makeup. Not every digital image produced by a computer is by virtue of that fact new per se, never mind noteworthy. It is possible to produce perfectly conventional films and photographs by digital means, and most of what is produced by digital media is not typical for the new possibilities of this medium. The only decisive question, therefore, is what images can be produced *only* with a computer, beyond what is usually done— and that, without a doubt, is the manipulable image, so-called animation. Digital media make images possible that allow the viewer, in the course of the viewing, to change the depicted object in a variety of ways. The viewer gains access to the imaginary image object. In this step the phenomenon of immersion has no role to play. If the computer screen shows horses, then these horses, given the right software and the right interface, can be made to run and jump. The medium allows for a previously unthinkable possibility of intervening in an imaginary, simply displayed world. Of course, it has always been possible to paint horses whichever way one liked. But digital techniques have made possible images in which the visible depiction can be modified *as* depiction. The result is a wholly new possibility of movement for image objects in an image, namely, willfully controllable movement. In a movie that displays a series of events, what happens is determined in advance. Yet if we elaborate a series of events in the imagination, that is by no means the case, for fantasies give themselves to the one fantasizing as not determined. It is precisely this openness of the unfolding of events that is also to be found in the possibility of modifying offered by computer animations. We are dealing with an animation in precisely those cases in which the displayed can be freely modified *as* displayed, and this means in those cases in which image objects assimilate themselves, in the way in which they can be modified, to the way in which fantasy contents can be modified. The imaginary object visible in the image in its flexibility has, by means of the new media, been structurally assimilated to the imaginary but invisible object of fantasy.

As mentioned earlier (see Chapter 2), Jean-Paul Sartre considers the painting of a house a kind of creation, albeit the creation of an imaginary house. The new media indeed allow for the construction of imaginary houses, of houses, that is, that can be inspected and walked around and that can be modified in the image as they can in fantasy. It is not until animation, really, that Sartre's thesis becomes convincing. Or, to put it differently, with Sartre it becomes particularly clear that phenomenological descriptions of the artificial presence of image objects take the easel picture to be some kind of rudimentary animation. The easel picture is understood to be a first, rather rough, attempt at employing the image not for referring semiotically but for producing something that is an imaginary thing sui generis. From this perspective art appears to be some sort of parallel endeavor to media studies, that is, as the attempt to investigate, in the medium of the image, the categorial possibilities of a medium. That is why artistic practice is of such relevance to the philosophy of the image. We have to go as far as saying that in retrospect the development of image media appears to be aimed at the constant improvement of the possibilities of the visible, imaginary image object to take on more and more the properties of the invisible, imaginary fantasy object. The invention of new image media today seems like an implicit search for ever better actualizations of the phenomenological understanding of the image. This view at least accords with the fact that hardly anyone besides the phenomenologist Vilém Flusser has seen, and partly foreseen, this process of assimilation of the image to fantasy. What is new about new media are not new perceptions but—as the title of the work of Flusser's that is authoritative in this respect formulates it—"A New Power of the Imagination." Human beings have always been able to picture things and events in their fantasy. But they had to do that by themselves. They have always been able to walk through the house they wanted to build for themselves in their fantasy. Yet now it becomes possible to have this tour through a house conceived by the digital image, or at least to have the image help in the conception. We can have a machine picture the images that we ourselves cannot conceive of, or at least cannot conceive of as quickly. Flusser, who likes to coin odd phrases, speaks—very appropriately in this case—of the user of a computer animation as an "imaginator [*Einbildner*]." We use the computer to imagine something, to have imaginations produced for us: "The images they imagine are not produced by them but by apparatuses, and that automatically."[7] Not least of all, it is its speed that endows this process with a new dimension: "Images then appear with breathtaking speed, one after the other, on the screen. We can watch this succession of images as if the power of the imagination [*Einbildungskraft*] had become independent, as if it had migrated from the internal to the external, as if we could watch our own dreams from the outside."[8]

It seems uncontroversial to claim that for such a phenomenological interpretation of the new media it is, in the end, completely insignificant what the inventors and producers of these technologies themselves want and think. The work, the images, are the topic of a phenomenological description. And yet—we simply have to admit it—it is a pleasant surprise or at least noteworthy when the creators in the conception of their new image technologies do not exactly aim at goals that directly contradict the phenomenological description. In the history of the development of digital media, the American Jaron Lanier is among the most important inventors and producers of simulation and cyberspace technologies. In 1990—that is, the same year Flusser publishes "A New Power of the Imagination"—he is asked what vision for the user he pursues with his many inventions. His answer is as short as it is unambiguous: "Eventually, you make your imagination external."[9] It is precisely this intended goal that constitutes a clear first qualitative jump in the development of the image by means of the new media: the image object becomes an externalized fantasy object. From this moment on, what becomes visible in the image is not only what someone has thought and conceived of but the process of imagining itself is transformed into the visible. We can see something we previously could only conceive of: we no longer depict products of fantasy but pictorially present the act of conceiving in the visible and, thereby, in public. What is at stake is an assimilation of the possibilities of modification of image objects to the possibilities of modification of the objects of one's own fantasy. Yet we have to stress that there remains an immense difference that concerns a particular phenomenological property of the imagination first described by Sartre. In protean fashion, fantasy contents are modifiable, but no change can surprise the one fantasizing. In fantasy no unexpected changes come about, none from which we could learn anything, none that could surprise us or even scare us. We cannot, for example, conceive of a dog and then be completely surprised by the imagined dog's being a poodle. For Sartre this property belongs to the four characteristics of the imagination: "As conception, I can easily and at my liking move such-and-such an object, turn a cube, make a plant grow, make a horse run, there will never be the smallest time-lag between the object and the consciousness. Not a second of surprise: the object that is moving is not alive, it *never precedes the intention.*"[10] Sartre has thus determined a characteristic of the imagination that will cause every attempt at a visible externalization of fantasy to fail. Only in the perceived world is there the phenomenon that a change has an effect of surprise on someone perceiving it. The visualization of freely imaginable changes makes these take on this property of the visible world. The freely controllable modifications on the computer screens may be as free as the fantasy contents, but in this respect they do not give themselves to the viewer as his or her own fantasies would. The imagination process translated by the computer into the visible allows for surprises. Precisely for this reason Flusser's description is so appropriate. In the end this description, which he notes almost as an aside, concerns a difference between his conceptions of the old and new power of the imagination: "And indeed: some of the images that light up in this way can surprise us: they are unexpected images."[11]

Simulation

The assimilation of image and imagination is the first milestone in the development of the new media; yet it is followed by a second. As paradoxical as it may sound, digital images acquire yet another new quality by means of an artificial retraction of the assimilation achieved; this second step back—a sort of "sublation" in the classical Hegelian sense of the term—takes place in the move from animation to simulation. If we ask whether the new media have created new images, we have to answer, "yes," and even twice already.

Let us imagine a computer on whose screen the user can have exclusively visible horses run. There are only two possibilities the computer can offer for modifying and moving the digitally generated horse. This is not an empirical statement but a logical one; only two kinds are thinkable. First, the computer can display on the screen a horse that is movable arbitrarily and without limits, a horse that can, by means of morphing, transition into any other shape whatsoever at any rate whatsoever. This is the case of animation. In a digital animation of this kind, the image object is completely without substance, without resistance and a freely available modeling mass without real mass. It is, literally, a surreal world.

Second, the computer may also generate on the screen a horse that possesses artificial properties. This horse then moves differently for the viewer, differently both from a horse on film and from the surreal horse. For this horse cannot be moved arbitrarily, as in fantasy, by the viewer. This horse, rather, behaves according to laws. Pick any video game as an example of this; there are horse-race video games in which the horses do not go as fast as we might want them to, in which different horses can do different things, and in which it may so happen that a stallion bolts off, without possibility of restraint, because on the neighboring pasture there is a, literally, attractive mare. It is only with this horse that we are dealing with a simulated horse because it possesses behavior. In simulations we do not have a surreal but a virtual world full of surprises. In the virtual reality of a digital simulation the viewer cannot do whatever he wants with the image objects; rather, he interacts with them. He can determine the movement of the pictorially displayed thing only within limits, for the image object, although it is a thing made of pure visibility, nonetheless possesses—in simulated fashion, precisely—material properties and thus is subject to an artificial physics. This physics that is artificially implemented in the image world can but does not have to be the physics of extrapictorial reality. Realities that do not exist can be simulated. The physics of the real world—confronted with virtual realities—is nothing more than a special case, for virtual things behave according to laws that are not necessarily those familiar from reality. Philosophically speaking, this means that the phenomenological description of images leads to a transcendental argument. The necessary condition of the possibility of thinking the plural of physics is that we presuppose simulation.

Independently of the question which reality it is that is simulated, in every case the simulation is a voluntary self-restraint and thereby constitutes yet another qualitative jump in the history of the image. For it is only here that a physics is artificially attached to imaginary image objects—and this means that although in the case of the simulation, too, we only look at images on a screen, we no longer look into a nonphysical sphere. Simulations are the artificial presence of a physics. The image object, which is detached from the laws of physics, is artificially materialized and thereby becomes a seemingly physical thing, even though that is not what it is and can never be, since it will always remain an image object. The concept of virtual reality, somewhat overused these days, should be reserved exclusively for to this particularly special phenomenon. Not every pictorial semblance is a virtual reality. A virtual reality is only given if the image no longer serves as a medium for referring to something absent, but rather if the image becomes a medium by means of which a particular kind of object is produced and presented—an object, that is, that is exclusively visible and yet, like a ghost, acts as if it had a substance and the properties of a substance.

In sum, all of this means that we can conceive of four kinds of image objects and that these possibilities of thought [*Denkmöglichkeiten*] are actualized, step by step, in the development of image media:

1. the fixed image object of the easel picture;
2. the moving, yet determined, image object of film;
3. the freely manipulable image object of animation; and
4. the interactive image object of simulation.

These types of images can be distinguished independently of the question of immersion. What is decisive about them is that they are conditioned exclusively by the image medium used in each case. This categorization, therefore, does not operate an evaluation; no claim to any kind of improvement or perfection in the new media is made. An animation is not a better film, and a simulation is not a better easel picture. Animation and simulation are different, and, seen historically, they are new image media—image media that, like the ones previously known, exist in immersive and nonimmersive form. Immersion is a property that can appear in all four kinds of pictorial visibility. *Trompe l'oeil* painting and panoramic images are examples of immersive easel paintings or at least of the attempt to create such immersive easel pictures. The many variations from 3D movies to IMAX exemplify the effort of linking immersion and film. Cyberspace provides immersive variants of animations and simulations.

In sum, all of this means that within the development of the new media two new forms of images need to be differentiated. Compared with animation, whose flexibility structurally resembles the type of movement of fantasies, visible movement in simulations, by virtue of its artificial, quasi-physical self-limitation seems to move away again from the imagination's kind of flexibility. We can think the way we want, but in simulations things no longer move just like we want—and it is this artificial retraction of the assimilation achieved that constitutes the unique relevance of digital media for epistemology, as well as for the future of the human.

Because in simulations the imaginary object is artificially subjected to a physics, it can become the object of scientific observation. This means concretely that in a simulation the imaginary image object becomes a visible object that can be used for scientific experiments. It has become a matter of course that the behavior of a car in accidents is tested largely in simulations on computer screens. But what does the concept of "testing" mean in this context? Obviously, the simulation does not conduct a real crash test. The simulation, rather, is an attempt to perfect an avenue of knowledge that—with the exception of Ernst Mach—has been relegated to a pitiable life in the shadows of the history of epistemology: the thought experiment, which for many epistemological theories is a contradiction in terms. Now the new media provide a unique implementation of the decidedly problematic phenomenon that is the thought experiment. For the simulation of modes of behavior in virtual realities is the implementation of a thought experiment as a virtual event: something is tried out, yet not in the empirical, but in the imaginary—albeit in a pictorially constituted imaginary. The goal this development aims at seems to be as paradoxical as any simulation: natural science without the observation of nature.[12] At this moment the computer is becoming increasingly a new kind of tool that can be used to actualize thought experiments that, without this amplifier of the imagination, would, in the truest sense of the term, be inconceivable: "Only when we concentrate on the images synthesized by computers . . . can we begin to have any idea at all what power of the imagination bursts forth here."[13] These new possibilities need image studies both for transcendental reflection and, equally, for social attention. For whether we regret or rejoice over the undoubtedly epochal step in the history of humanity constituted by the new images, we can no longer stop or even reverse this process.

Plato's Concept of Mimesis and Its Concealed Canon

Even though most theories of the image claim to address images in *all* their various manifestations, that is by no means always the case. All too often, only certain genres, image media, or even just concrete works of art are considered, even though one talks about the image in general. This concentration on parts of the whole usually has no further problematic consequences. If the context of an image theory is known or if an introduction explains which images are considered to be canonical, the reader knows what the propositions of the text refer to. This knowledge, however, is necessary: only in that way can the theory be adequately understood. Who would want to doubt that it is easier to understand a text when it is known what the text is about? For this reason the reading of theories of the image, but of art as well, becomes very problematic if the canonical works are unknown to the reader. This is by no means the rule, but it can happen, for example, when theories of the image and of art are very old, when the convincing paradigmatic examples to which the theory could have referred when it was first elaborated are no longer familiar, or when translations of central concepts lead to shifts in meaning. In all cases it holds true that a theory of the image, and also of art, that refers to an unknown canon of works is hardly comprehensible; and conversely, the interpretational determination of a concealed conceived canon is an indispensable hermeneutic step toward understanding a philosophy of art. This is the very situation in which we find ourselves when we engage one of the most famous philosophies of the image and of art in the West: Plato's theory of mimesis, particularly as he elaborates it in Book X of the *Republic.*

Plato's reputation as a philosopher of the image and of art is not the best; on the contrary, his theses are as infamous as they are famous. Commentators like to look at Book X of the *Republic* as a scandal of the history of philosophy because here, it is alleged, Plato, the most venerated of all classics, blatantly calls for the statutory prohibition of art, even worse: not just for the prohibition of art but for the prohibition of the production of any images whatsoever. And indeed, the text serves as the theoretical foundation of the numerous image prohibitions enacted in Western history. Sir Karl Popper sees in Book X of the *Republic* just another proof for his basic opinion that Plato, in his philosophy as a whole, is a protofascist dictatorial enemy of the open society.[1]

This radical and sobering interpretation of Plato as iconoclast and despiser of art is undoubtedly correct if Plato, in those passages that speak of art and images, wants to address those objects that we today associate with these concepts, for example sculptures by Frank Stella, which are art, and the news on TV, which displays images. Yet the question is whether that is the case. Why can it be supposed that that is what Plato wants to do? Just because the text speaks of art and of images? Perhaps Plato is an example of the case suggested above, where general propositions in the end refer to only one canon. It could therefore make sense to embark on a path of interpretation, an interpretation in which the tables are turned, so to speak. Such an interpretation would not read Plato in order to find out what he says about art but exclusively as if we did not know what things his reflections in Book X are about, in order to think afterward about which phenomena fit what he says, and for which phenomena what he says makes sense. What is the topic of Book X, actually? What phenomena could someone have in mind who writes what Plato writes? Answering these questions might lead us to successfully reconstruct a canon that is perhaps concealed in Plato's theory of art and of images. We would suppose he is correct and then ask, *For what phenomena is what he says correct?* This would be a decidedly hermeneutic way of proceeding. One of the few applicable principles to be found developed in the many reflections on hermeneutics says that something can only be understood if it is presupposed at the outset that the unintelligible that is to be made intelligible makes sense. Without credit, that is, without a supposition, granted in advance, that a text makes sense, no text whatsoever can be understood as having sense. To suppose that Plato wants to summarily prohibit art—which today also means Picasso, Poussin, and Michelangelo—and summarily to prohibit images—which today must include vacation photos, video clips, and posters as well—two and a half millennia later, at least, has little sense. In short, it is worth a try to read Book X with a supposition that allows for sense to be possible, that is, with the supposition that what is written there makes sense and is correct if only we know what this book is about—if we know what, for Plato, were canonical works of art and of pictorial imitation.

What is Plato talking about?

The search for the objects that go along with Plato's theses, of course, builds on the hope that Plato's argumentation is particularly appropriate and makes sense for those rare works of art and very subtle forms of imitation that, for good reasons, were and had to be canonical for him—which is not yet to say that Plato's theses are correct. "Making sense" and "being correct" are two distinct categories that reveal one of the central problems of Plato's text: if Plato really were a theoretical despiser of art and an iconoclast, then we would find amassed in Book X sentences of which we would have to say not only that they are wrong but also that they do not make sense—and that's a difference. We have to go as far as saying that if we really are to suppose that in Book X Plato—although he, unfortunately, suggests just this—philosophizes about images, then his text borders on mental derangement. Three exemplary passages provide proof of such a view.

First example: in Schleiermacher's translation Socrates asks his interlocutor: "Do you think that someone who could make both the thing imitated and its shadow image [*Schattenbild*] would allow himself to be serious about making shadow images and put this at the forefront of his life as the best thing to do?—No, I don't.—I suppose that, if he truly had knowledge of the things he imitates, he'd be much more serious about actions than about imitations of them."[2] Plato claims here that one imitates an object because he or she is not capable of actually producing this object. This proposition, however, is not only wrong but—if it were meant as it now seems—completely foreign to reality: somebody who paints a chair hardly paints it because he or she is not talented enough to produce an actual chair. The same holds true for Plato's reflection that whoever is capable of producing the original is most competent at producing the imitation.[3] This, too, is completely inapt, as if a watchmaker could produce the best images of watches. Andreas Schubert's perfectly appropriate commentary on these passages of the *Republic* reads: "Is the good painter of a chair at the same time dealer and producer of furniture, physicist, 'office creature'? This is just as difficult to make believable as is, generally, that anyone could come up with suppositions of this kind. In reference to painting, in any case, Plato's claim is crude."[4]

Second example: Socrates summarizes his reflections: Is it not "as we were saying just now, a painter, though he knows nothing about cobblery, can make what seems to be a cobbler to those who know as little about it as he does?"[5] Here Plato claims that whoever imitates a shoe engages in an activity that is held to be the production of a shoe, and completely consciously so. He would thus imitate something in order for a later viewer to take the imitation for what is imitated. Yet again what was said for the first example holds true: if this claim were about images, we would let Plato utter the obvious absurdity that a painter creates something we are to regard as the original. Yet how can it be supposed that Plato could really have believed that the painter of a shoe would want his image to be regarded as a real pair of shoes?

Third example: Socrates elaborates on the methods he deems appropriate for unmasking an imitation to be such. He asks rhetorically: "And don't measuring, counting, and weighing give us most welcome assistance in these cases, so that we aren't ruled by something's looking bigger, smaller, more numerous, or heavier, but by calculation, measurement, or weighing?—Of course."[6] Plato's methods are unambiguous: measuring, counting, weighing; we could also say they are the methods of measurement of physics. Once more, however, the proposition seems more than absurd if referred to images. Anyone who would want to prove that a photo of Peter is an image and not the real Peter would have to take a measuring tape to measure the length of Peter on the photo paper. He or she would be pleasantly surprised to find that the imitated Peter measures an inch while the real Peter measures six feet. Therefore, the imitated Peter is not the real Peter, who, by the way, also weighs 190 pounds, unlike the image—what nonsense.

Phenomenological excursus: Imitation, depiction, and copy

What consequences can we draw from these three passages? Two are possible: either Plato is confused, or he does not speak of images in the usual sense. There are no other possibilities, and it is worth a try to take a closer look at the second possibility. This means we must—as announced—ask whether there is a phenomenon in whose case the propositions of Plato's just presented at least make sense. With this reversed questioning the beginning of Book X becomes important because there Plato himself elaborates on the question of his topic. Thus he says at the very beginning that in Book X he undertakes answering the question *What is mimesis?* Having called for a prohibition of art in Books II and III, but precisely only called for it, in Book X, which seems a little like an artificial addition, he wants to make up for not having justified such a prohibition earlier by now answering the question *What is mimesis?* The argumentation is decidedly epistemological: if we know what mimesis is, we will understand why art and images should be prohibited.

Schleiermacher translates Plato's opening question as follows: "Could you tell me what depiction in general is?"[7] And this, precisely, takes us to a point that may easily get us off on the wrong track. Modern image theory has the means to show that *depiction* is a mistranslation of *mimesis* that entails grave consequences. This mistranslation not only makes it difficult to recognize Plato's concealed conception of a canon but even renders it unrecognizable.[8] For "mimesis" is a genus; it corresponds to a wide concept of imitation. This, however, means that at least two different phenomena fall under the concept of "mimesis" or "imitation": on the one hand, the phenomenon of imitation by depiction and, on the other, the phenomenon of imitation by copying or replication; these two forms, and this is the intention of this excursus, can be differentiated.

An imitation is an object that in certain respects bears resemblance to another thing. This in turn means that the imitation object and the imitated object possess partially identical properties. For something to bear a resemblance means that it is partially identical with something else. Thus, for example, twins often look so much alike that even their parents mistake one for the other. This, however, also shows us that not every thing that bears resemblance to another thing has to be an imitation of this other thing. Twins are not imitations even though they very much resemble one another. Only if something more joins resemblance can we, in the case of two resembling things, speak of a relation of imitation. This further characteristic is intention: imitations are artifacts deliberately produced for the sake of resemblance. An object becomes an imitation only if and when resemblance was intended in a process of production, if the resemblance was one of the reasons why the object was constructed the way it was constructed. This, by the way, is also why a cloned human being, who is an artificially produced twin, has to be called an imitation.

On this basis we can now distinguish two kinds of imitation, for there are two possibilities of how resemblance can be generated artificially. Depictions and copies both artificially produce resemblances, yet each does so in a fundamentally different way. To differentiate these two ways, we must take note that it is possible to describe an image's resemblance to what is depicted only if the depicting material is distinguished from the displayed depiction; for it is not, obviously, the material image carrier that bears resemblance to the depicted object. The material of an image can be oil on canvas or photo paper, yet these do not resemble that to which an image may be referred. The only phenomena that are decisive are those that seem to be visibly present in the viewing, the image objects, for these are viewed when an image is referred, as a sign, to something it resembles. The object that becomes visible on the image surface bears resemblance to an existent or fictitious material object. That is why we can say that in an image it is not something actual that resembles something else but something appears to a viewer to resemble something else. And this, precisely, is what is different in the case of the copy. For in the case of the copy we are indeed dealing with the kind of imitation in which a material object is to possess physical resemblance to another material object. How striking a difference with the image this marks becomes obvious when we compare, for example, the photo and the copy, or replica, of a watch. The relation of resemblance in each case is fundamentally different. In both cases we are dealing with the imitation of a watch, but only the replica tries to be that which it imitates. The replica Rolex is a watch, while the image of a Rolex is not a watch. This is precisely what is essential to copies or replicas: they lead to the production of objects that are regarded by the viewer as examples of the kinds of objects they imitate. The copy tries, by means of material resemblance, to duplicate an object in its very existence. This, however, is not at all the intention of a depiction. Depiction is concerned with creating an object on which an image object appears for the viewer, an image object that, in a physical sense, is not present at all. In the case of the copy, however, both relata of the relation of resemblance are physically existent. This entails that there can be no copies of fictitious things: there are only images but no copies of Martians.

The copy as critical measure

This distinction of imitation, image, and copy provides the conceptual tools for returning to the problem introduced at the beginning of this chapter: what phenomenon did Plato have in mind as archetypical example in his critique of mimesis? The answer—at least for the moment—appears to be unequivocal: copies. Book X of the *Republic* is so difficult a text to understand because Plato has to think and write with a wide concept of mimesis that equivocally names two phenomena that for his purposes, precisely, he would have had to differentiate. In Book X an equivocal concept is not yet recognized and reflected on in its equivocality; it belongs to an early phase of philosophical argumentation in which necessary differentiations have not yet been completed. For whenever Plato speaks of mimesis, two very different forms of mimesis are confused. Schleiermacher translates the guiding question from Book X as "Could you tell me what depiction in general is?" This gives rise to the impression that Plato is concerned with depictions, and this is, on the one hand, simply wrong and, on the other, very unfortunate. The translation is wrong because *mimesis* refers to all kinds of imitation, and the *pars pro toto* is unfortunate because the wrong part, precisely, of the two kinds of imitation is elevated to the status of the whole, that part for which Plato's reflections precisely do not work. We can say that the translation attracts attention to the wrong canonical works. For the text becomes much more understandable if we start from the idea that Plato does not criticize the production of depictions but only that of bad copies. For him the copy is the canonical form of imitation. If we refer Book X to bad copies and look at it independently of its being coerced into a metaphysical system, it is endowed with a high degree of phenomenological and psychological descriptive force. The passages already mentioned, which appear devoid of sense when referred to images, suddenly gain evidentiary force if we suppose that for Plato copies or replicas are the canonical form of imitation. We can enumerate the points that speak for this thesis as follows:

1. Copies—unlike images—until this day retain the negative aftertaste that, according to Plato, all imitations leave behind.

2. Copies often really are forgery, illusion, make-believe, and deceit, as Plato time and again claims for mimesis.

3. Over against the original, copies are indeed, as Plato writes, considered secondary. This is not the case for images; they are, on the contrary, often preferred to the reality that is pictured.

4. Plato's thesis that someone who imitates something wants to create something that is supposed to be taken for the original unambiguously applies only to copies and is wrong in the case of images.

5. Plato supposes that a mimesis would not be produced if the original could be produced. This applies to the makers of replicas who indeed only copy something because they are not capable of creating something on a par with the original.

6. This goes along with Plato's always arguing in such a way as if copies were easier to produce than the originals. This is wrong in the case of images but applies in the case of copies.

7. Plato adds the further reproach that someone who owns copies would rather possess the original object that is imitated. For images this thesis is entirely inapt. For copies it is not logically necessary, either, but it does describe a widespread psychological phenomenon: many owners of a replica Rolex would rather own a real Rolex.

8. The methods Plato lists for the unmasking of the deceit of imitations, very appropriately, are the methods current in revealing copies and replicas to be such: Plato speaks of measuring, counting, weighing. A Rolex replica can usually be recognized by weighing or by counting the

stones in the clockwork. Copies, just as Plato describes, are revealed to be such by means of scientific methods.

9. Plato's comparison, not mentioned so far, of the artist with someone who holds up a mirror shows that for him mimesis cannot be a form of depiction. Even by means of a mirror it is not possible to see anything depicted but only something that is really present. Mirror images are not images since they display no image object. Rather, they direct, by optical mediation, our gaze onto a real object. What we see in the mirror, we treat, as is the case for the copy, as an object in attendance—and rightly so: in the case of the mirror we can be sure that we do not see artificially present things but objects that are really in attendance. Just as it cannot be copied, a Martian cannot be seen in a mirror.

10. Finally, the most important point, Plato's supposed outrageous intention that has so often caused tempers to flare, and which Plato seeks to justify with his theory of mimesis: the artist is to be prosecuted under criminal law. This is, of course, a horrifying idea if we think of the artist as the visual artist; yet if the canonical idea is that of makers of copies, we have to say that the prohibition of mimesis has nothing dictatorial about it but rather, on the contrary, constitutes common practice under the rule of law. The fabrication of copies and replicas is prohibited under the rule of law as well. A designer who comes up with a design for a new chair because he or she had an idea of what a good chair can be has this design protected, and not a few designers who have their designs plagiarized by uninspired colleagues wish to see these makers of copies punished.

The image as copy

Plato's criticism becomes convincing when it is referred not to images but to cheap and unimaginative copies and replicas. If Plato spoke of the reprehensibility of such copies, his concern would at least be understandable. Yet the problem is this: he does not speak of those! The thesis that Plato is a critic of copies cannot be the last word but only an intermediary result in the interpretation of Book X. For this thesis suffers from the simple yet grave problem that Plato in the text explicitly extends his criticism to images. Everywhere he speaks of *eikon* and *eidola* and thus uses those concepts that are rightly translated by the word *image*. The reading of Book X proposed here thus must not conceal that with his concept of mimesis Plato means both forms of imitation and that he refers what he claims about these two forms always also to images. For these reasons we *cannot* read Plato as if his canon simply included bad copies alone; the situation is more complicated. We cannot understand Plato's argumentation as a pure criticism of copies even though he criticizes what he criticizes as if it were a copy. Yet this, precisely, is the decisive point: he criticizes something that is not a copy but presents itself as a copy for doing so—and this something, for him, is the image. This, however, can impossibly be all images, for the least number of images is treated as copies or even taken for copies. There must have been an idea of a canon that corresponds to the equivocal concept of mimesis—any other solution cannot endow the text with sense. This means that for Plato images must be canonical that are produced and treated as copies or replicas. Only when he refers to such subtle and rare images can he at the same time talk about images and yet meaningfully reject them with the criteria of a criticism of copies. This, no doubt, is a convoluted solution but his argumentation calls for it: Plato treats all forms of mimesis as if they were copies even though some—images, precisely—are not copies. This means that his canon must consist of rare hybrid works that are copies or replicas as much as they are images, in whose case replication and depiction converge—in the concept as in reality. This follows from the sense of the concept: since Plato works with a concept of mimesis that combines depiction and copy, the works that are canonical for him must be such that this convergence of the different is the case empirically as well, must be works in whose case depiction and replication are given in an object. Only if we suppose that his reflections in Book X are about such esoteric objects that, even though they are images, nonetheless also present themselves as copies does the text become coherent. Complicated as this solution sounds, it is all the more simple from the point of view of art history. For it is remarkable that when we want to determine the works that are canonical for Plato's theory, it suffices to ask what the greatest and most significant work of art was in Plato's time and his hometown, and we will quickly have *the* archetypical example for a depiction that is treated as a copy: the *Athena Parthenos.*

Athena Parthenos

Approximately forty feet high, the *Athena Parthenos* is a religious sculpture of gold and ivory created by Phidias that was set up in the *cella* of the Parthenon temple on the Acropolis. Only massively reduced Roman copies—such as the second century's so-called *Varvakeion Athena*, about three feet high, now in the National Archaeological Museum in Athens— provide a faint reflection of this masterpiece of High Classicism. On her extended right hand alone, Athena carried a seven-foot statue of Nike. A significant part of the Delian League's treasure in gold was attached— albeit detachable—to the statue.

But what is significant for the philosophical argument in Book X of the *Republic* is not the impressive size of the *Athena Parthenos* but the function of this sculpture and the way in which it was treated by Athenians. The *Athena Parthenos* was an idol [*Kultbild*] that was ritually exalted and had sacrifices made to it, which speaks to a certain understanding of imitation that was essential to Greek religious practice. For the way in which an idol in a temple was interpreted in the Greece of classical antiquity is fundamentally distinct from the Christian interpretation of an image of Christ in a church. A temple is not a church. This difference concerns not only the exterior appearance but the concepts themselves. Both *temple* and *church* denote houses of God but very different ones. According to Greek understanding, the house of God is the House of the God; that is, it is his house, and he is present there. If we wanted, we could loosely say that the Greek gods live in their temples. The temple is never a house of God in which worship of God could take place; it is the house that belongs to the god himself, that which is dedicated to him. For this reason worship in classical Greece always took place in front of the temple in the holy precinct, the so-called *temenos*. For the Christian religion, however, the church is a house in which the congregation meets to celebrate services together. The Christian church develops from the basilica, a market hall that serves as a place of congregation. To this fundamental difference in the understanding of the house of God corresponds an equally fundamental difference in the understanding of the depictions of gods. The depiction of a god in a Greek temple's *cella* is not interpreted by the Greeks as an aide for contemplation that helps to better relate to the god in prayer but as the artistic attempt to let the god become present. The depiction of a god in antiquity is not a sign that refers but a presentation in the literal sense of the word.[9] What is at stake is the artificial creation of presence: artificially produced presentness. And this presenting takes place in the sculpture, which is thus conceived of not as an image but as a surrogate. The sculpture does not refer to the god; it is divine presence. We could say that precisely that which, from a Christian perspective, was usually condescendingly reviled as idolatry, from a Greek perspective was an un-problematic normality to be embraced. We do need to add, however, that the very interpretation of Greek religious practice as a form of image wor-ship is precisely an interpretation from an external perspective that only non-Greeks can give, for the Greeks from their perspective did precisely not think of themselves as worshipping an image but as worshipping a god. Greeks do not offer sacrifices to a sculpture but to a God present in the sculpture. In short, in this cultural context it is self-evident that the idol is what it imitates, and this means, without any hint of blasphemy, that from a phenomenological point of view the Greek idol is a copy of a god. What is at stake is not the production of a semblance of something but the artificial creation of real presence.[10]

And it is precisely against this background that in its formal elabo-ration the *Athena Parthenos* is equally avant-garde, extravagant, and pro-vocative. For the manner in which Phidias created this depiction of the goddess, while staying within the style of such depictions, revolts against the idea of treating images as copies. We have to realize that the *Athena Parthenos*, along with the sculpture of Zeus in Olympia (the most impor-tant depiction of a god in Greek classical antiquity), contains within itself a fundamental criticism of this religion because the image in its proportions refuses to conform to the principle of mimesis as copy that the contempo-rary image of a god demands. Phidias is—very probably—the first artist in the West to consciously break the biunique size relations of original and figurative image [*Urbild und Abbild*]. He introduces into sculpture the idea, so taken for granted today, that a sculpture must create something that becomes visible, exclusively visible, that is, through the sculpture but that might stand in contradiction to the actually fabricated body of the sculpture. Measured by the proportions of the human, Phidias formed the head of the *Athena Parthenos* too big. Yet since as a normal viewer one could only see the head at a height of forty feet, it looked smaller to the viewer. Phidias formed the head larger than human proportion prescribes with the effect that the head up high cannot appear too small to the viewer down below—and there we have it, the decisive word: *appear*.

Phidias introduces the world of appearances into the world of religious presence. From an art historical perspective this is an eminently important step. For Phidias shows in his mode of proceeding that he no longer wants to serve only and exclusively the theological task he has been ascribed. For this must be said in all clarity: from the point of view of theology, and from Plato's point of view, Phidias's step is pure blasphemy. He gives his Athena a hydrocephalus; this, Plato would say, can be measured. Yet for a reading of Book X this means that Plato's idea that a bad imitation can be shown to be such by means of measuring becomes quite understandable against the background of this scandal. His opinion is the expression of a position that is as desperate as it is conservative: Plato perceives the step that consists in grasping the depiction of a god as an autonomous artistic sculpture—that is, as a depiction and not as a religious presentation—to be a step in the wrong direction. Plato, progressive and critical of theology as he may be in his philosophy, remains completely attached to traditional theological thinking in his concept of mimesis, which can be seen in his anger about the *Athena Parthenos*. Plato's concept of mimesis corresponds to the theological concerns of classical cult works. For Plato, too, art does not have the task of producing a new or independent, never mind an autonomous, object. It is rather to deliver a piece-by-piece reproduction that is as precise as possible. In Book IV already, Plato articulates the thesis that an imitation that succeeds as a whole does not come about by the artist's having the whole in mind but by each part of the thing to be imitated being separately imitated as precisely as possible:

Suppose, then, that someone came up to us while we were painting a statue and objected that, because we had painted the eyes (which are the most beautiful part) black rather than purple, we had not applied the most beautiful colors to the most beautiful parts of the statue. We'd think it reasonable to offer the following defense: "You mustn't expect us to paint the eyes so beautifully that they no longer appear to be eyes at all, and the same with the other parts. Rather you must look to see whether by dealing with each part appropriately, we are making the whole statue beautiful."[11]

This means that according to Plato's understanding of mimesis an imitation must be determined in its entire appearance [*Erscheinung*] exclusively by the appearance [*Aussehen*] of its parts. The individual parts are imitated as if they alone were to be imitated and as if they were not parts of a whole. The appearance of the parts for Plato thus is not to be determined contextually, that is, in the entire appearance. This is an idea that, first, is convincing for copies and replicas and, second, is extraordinarily consistent when seen against the background of the doctrine of ideas. For every part of a whole also has, like the whole, an idea and is, therefore, to be treated on a par with the whole.

Stage sets

Thanks to its theological function, art in Plato's time suggested reducing the concept of mimesis to the copy—though this applies only to canonical components—and taking the step, difficult to understand today and still wrong in its generality, of treating all images as copies. Against the example of the *Athena Parthenos*, however, we might want to raise the point that we are dealing with a spatial sculpture and not an easel painting. Yet a sculpture is always already a form of imitation that in certain respects possesses a slight parentage with copies because it does not construct a space of illusion but really presents a spatial body.[12] We could also object that in the end this example does not help us understand how Plato could come to take the step of treating images as copies, for in this example, not an image in the narrow sense but a sculpture is treated as a copy. From within this perspective Plato's allegations against painters, that they want to copy and not depict, still remain inappropriate. For painting, as well, we must thus ask what variants Plato had in mind and whether there might not be among these some idiosyncratic exceptional and hybrid phenomena to which what he says applies. If that be the case, a reader who approaches Plato's text hermeneutically may yet discover a sense in its understanding of the image.

Painting in the fourth century BC was indeed highly developed as illusionistic in a specific purposive context: that of painting stage sets. The stage set, however, is a very special image because it is an image within an image. Plato's claims about mimesis apply to the painting of stage sets in principle, no matter what these paintings might have actually looked like.[13] The painted house in the background of a stage is treated by the actors as if it were not a painted house but a real one. When an actor says,

"Go into the house!" and points at the set that is the house, then he and the spectator take the image to be what it merely depicts. This, however, means that what Plato reflects on theoretically is put into practice: the image is treated as a copy. For the spectator and the actor, the image is supposed to be what it displays and not an image of what it displays—and this holds even if we can clearly see that the stage set is an image.

If against the background of these properties of stage settings we additionally call to mind that, according to Plato's metaphysics, perceptible reality as a whole is itself just a figurative image of a world of ideas, then this means that for Plato every normal image is an image in an image. The stage set had to be canonical for him because there we find exemplified what from the point of view of the doctrine of ideas really holds for every image. The normal visible world is itself already an image of the ideas, that is, it is a kind of stage on which ideas display themselves. Hence, for Plato the "normal" painted images are always already images on a great stage. The stage set is only the evident clarification of this general situation. It is thus quite obvious that this particular form of images had to be canonical for Plato, especially since vase painting, highly developed as well, never had the goal Plato is concerned with in his argument: namely to copy.

Mimesis eikastike and *mimesis phantastike*

To sum up: Plato criticizes the use of images as copies that is indeed made of contemporary religious sculpture and painted stage sets [*Kult- und Bühnenbilder*]. The proper aesthetic value of artistic elaboration as it is known and by and large appreciated today is not thematized by Plato because he measures every work of art against that form of imitation that for him is the definitive, canonical form of imitation: the perfect, 100 percent copy. This allows us to claim, furthermore, that in Plato we have the example of a philosopher who produces grave problems of understanding by talking about imitation while thinking merely about canonical works. Such an interpretation does not dispute that Book X of the *Republic* suffers from not having explicitly distinguished conceptually between mimesis as copy and mimesis as depiction. Plato could have formulated his thesis much more precisely and made it less prone to misunderstanding if he had had this conceptual distinction available to him. This is of course a

shortcoming, and especially for a philosopher, if by philosophy we understand the labor on and with concepts. Thus the *Republic*, so to speak, passes on a problem of differentiation; it leaves behind a problem of distinction
that must be solved. The question is, *Where and when in the history of the
philosophy of the image was the explicit conceptual distinction between copy
and depiction captured clearly for the first time?*

It's almost too good to be true: in Plato. Plato himself makes the
differentiation in question and shows himself rightly to be the classic of
all classics after all. The explanation for this unexpected answer is simple.
Approximately ten years after the *Republic*, in his dialogue *The Sophist*,
which he writes sometime between 366 and 361 BC, Plato reengages with
the concept of mimesis, very briefly yet extraordinarily profitably.[14] Once
more Plato seems to refer to Phidias's *Athena Parthenos*. Yet in this renewed
attempt to describe, this time conceptually as well, what is reprehensible
about Phidias's particular kind of imitation, Plato makes the distinction
between *mimesis eikastike* and *mimesis phantastike*. He now writes, "I see
two types of the art of imitation here too."[15] He describes the first kind of
imitation, the *mimesis eikastike*, as follows: "One type of imitation I see
is the art of likeness-making. That's the one we have whenever someone
produces an imitation by keeping to the proportions of length, breadth,
and depth of his model, and also by keeping to the appropriate colors of
its parts."[16] It appears rather clearly what sort of phenomenon Plato here
addresses as *mimesis eikastike*. Schleiermacher translates the term as *eben-
bildnerische Kunst* or "art of likeness-making." This is very appropriate.
The term corresponds to the perhaps somewhat more modern concept
of the copy: when we build a likeness, we build a copy or replica. Yet
the point that is decisive systematically only follows the prior definition
of likeness-making as a question. Plato has Theaetetus ask the question:
"But don't all imitations try to do that?"[17] We thus read the very question a reader of the *Republic* must ask him- or herself, for there we did
indeed get the impression that all imitations have the goal of producing
copies or replicas and that images cannot achieve this. Yet this thesis no
longer seems appropriate even to Plato but rather seems to render absolute, render as a whole a specific form of imitation. He, too, sees that not
all imitations strive for a *mimesis eikastike*. That is why he determines a
second kind of imitation by giving an example that can be interpreted as

a further reference to the *Athena Parthenos*: "But don't all imitations try to do that?—Not the ones who sculpt or draw very large works. If they reproduced the true proportions of their beautiful subjects, you see, the upper parts would appear smaller than they should, and the lower parts would appear larger, because we see the upper parts from farther away and the lower parts from closer."[18] Plato calls this kind of imitation, of which he rightly says that it "is quite significant for painting and for the rest of imitation,"[19] *mimesis phantastike*. What he means is the phenomenon of depiction. Something is not measurably similar but appears to the viewer as similar. Plato has thus achieved the conceptual differentiation lacking in the *Republic*. The differentiation of the concept of mimesis in the two concepts *mimesis eikastike* and *mimesis phantastike* appears to be a particularly meaningful suggestion—even if it were only terminological. For the differentiation by means of adjectival additions indicates that without further determination mimesis is an equivocal concept that can be differentiated into two phenomena; this is not the case for "image" and "copy." We cannot tell, on the face of it, that they are subordinate concepts to the concept of imitation.

This conceptual distinction allows us to precisely determine Plato's canonical case of a reprehensible imitation. Plato discards, and this may cause one last surprise, not the *mimesis eikastike*, that is, not as we might think the planned production of a perfect copy, but the *mimesis phantastike*, whose Greek term Schleiermacher for this reason translates as *Trugbildnerei*, or making of false appearances.[20] This evaluation, which we would not expect because we might think that both a classification and an appreciation would go along with the positivization of the principles of depicting, is extremely consistent. On reading Book X of the *Republic* we might easily get the impression, even though that is not written there, that Plato would not consider a perfect likeness, that is, an imitation that cannot be revealed as such by measuring, weighing, and counting, to be possible. He indeed does not take this to be possible if we take depictions to create artificial presence. In this we can only agree with him: images cannot create likenesses. But what about when there is no production of images but of real copies that perfectly withstand all scientific tests, that cannot be shown to be forgeries—precise, indistinguishable likenesses? This ideal case that can never be attained with images is not considered by Plato to be reprehensible but, on the contrary, extraordinarily desirable. For what other reason (if indeed he had, as it seems in the *Republic*, really been against imitating as copying) would he have evaluated Phidias's step of precisely not copying but depicting to be bad and not positive? Why does he not say, as it would be common with a modern art canon, that Phidias's sculpture is better than a shop window mannequin because Phidias does not even try to copy or replicate? Yet this is precisely what Plato sees differently. A mannequin for him would be the better imitation because he treats all imitations as if they wanted to copy or replicate. This is the decisive point and Plato's great shortcoming, which arises from his rendering absolute of a special canon. We are not justified in most cases to reproach images with being bad copies. An image is no more a bad copy than it is a bad car. It is no copy at all but a depiction. The concept "copy" cannot be applied to images at all. Yet since Plato's very special canon really included the rather rare cases of idols and stage sets, he could, guided by these special cases, evaluate images as bad copies. This only works with images that really enter into competition with copies and replicas—and those are the only ones criticized by Plato. For him they are images that in the end are in competition with philosophical activity itself.

The criticism of mimesis from the *Republic* continues in the *Sophist*, albeit conceptually more precisely, for it determines the reason why images, when they are compared to copies, are inferior. (This comparison suggests itself only for idols and stage sets.) For this inferiority is not obvious. Plato does not clearly name the real reason for his disdain until the *Sophist*. The coming-about of the image is perforce connected to the introduction of a viewer's perspective, and it is this perspective, precisely, that does not exist in the case of copies. Copies are correct imitations from all points of view, and Plato thinks positively of this. They can, if they are good, withstand every scientific testing, every weighing, counting, and measuring. The image, however, is a correct imitation only from one perspective and therefore only from one specific viewer's point of view. The viewer of a painting must stand upright in front of the canvas; the viewer of the *Athena Parthenos* must stand on the temple floor: "If the image were not seen from the angle intended, it would in no way resemble the original."[21] What is depicted only appears to be reproduced correctly "because," Plato writes, "it is seen from the appropriate point of view."[22]

Yet if the viewer "came to be able to see such a thing adequately," he or she would see that it "would seem unlike the thing it claims to be like."[23] Plato realizes that every production and viewing of images is bought at the dear price of a point of view, for points of view have the disadvantage of contingency. The freedom and independence from points of view of the copy, however, is an ideal for Plato, which is why in the *Sophist* he interprets copying as an activity that is related to philosophical activity. For Plato, what the copyist and the philosopher have in common is that they try to refer to something without interpreting this something in a contingent manner. There is no mediating grammar of picturing between copy and what is copied, no perspective of transformation, no distorting style, no language, no medium.

This, for Plato, should be the philosopher's model: to produce an imitation of reality that, like the copy, is correct not only from a human perspective. It is the ideal of a detachment from points of view, a detachment we can also address in the literal sense as a striving for the absolute. Such an imitation can make the claim to knowledge. Plato criticizes images and theories that pretend to be more than they are, that is, mere theories, with the same arguments. He compares sophistry with *mimesis phantastike* not because it elaborates a theory of the world from a certain point of view but because it passes off a point of view as truth, because it makes us overlook its own pictoriality, because it creates images that interpret but are not to be recognized as interpreting images. What is devastating is only the confusion that takes place when an image—that is, a contingent way of seeing—is taken to be a truth. Against this background it must seem profitable to Plato if—as is the case today for every normal viewing of images—a copy is recognized and treated as such. A theory or an imitation that can rightly lay claim to truth for Plato must not make us overlook that it is an artificial theory or an artificial imitation. Yet precisely this call for truthfulness can be interpreted as a paradox internal to Plato's concept of mimesis, as the studies of Iris Därmann, in particular, have been able to show: "The maker of likenesses must picture perfectly in order to achieve a non-perfect mimesis that identifies itself as such, while the appearance-making illusionist without exception engages in bad, imprecise mimesis in order to bring about a perfect pictoriality, a pictoriality, that is, that is not recognizable as pictoriality. . . . The non-imitation thus turns out to be a perfect imitation because the perfect imitation is no longer an imitation."[24]

But this also means that neither the viewing of images as images nor, *a forteriori*, the viewing of copies is reprehensible for Plato; what is reprehensible is exclusively the categorial confusion that takes place when images are viewed as copies, exemplary in the case of idols and stage sets and, figuratively, in the case of sophistry. In the religious cult and on the stage, from Plato's point of view, something passes itself off as a copy and yet is but an image. That has devastating effects, namely the same effects the sophists have with their theories: contingent points of view are presented as truth, or, put differently, rhetoric passes itself off as philosophy. And there seems to be only one way not to succumb to this sophistic danger of confusion: the flight forward. Heinrich Niehues-Pröbsting's important work underscores that the insight into its own problematic, related to that of art, demands of philosophy "that it does not pass off the image as the thing but recognizably as an image."[25] Thus, in the end Plato indeed leads us to a decidedly modern thought, we could say, to the demand always to combine philosophy with a media-theoretical self-reflection. Plato's reflections on mimesis formulate a precise perspective for philosophical activity. In order not to become sophistry, philosophical reflection must lay open and thematize the means that enable these reflections, since to attempt an overcoming of its own mediality, its own being tied to language, for Plato is no perspective. If a philosopher wants to communicate, he or she cannot dispense with a medium of depiction; but that does not mean he or she has to deny it. On the contrary, the mimetic character of philosophy demands of philosophy itself "a consistent co-thematization of that mediality through which something is formed and said such that a knowledge is always remembered, the knowledge that what comes to the fore with the 'means' of speech or of the image is not the thing itself but the depiction of the thing."[26]

What Are Media?

When we look at the current state of media studies, we might well think that it may be better not to ask the question *What are media?* but rather *What isn't a medium?* Indeed the situation seems to be such that media studies is determined by a rather large number of concepts of media that are, however, equally wide, in part even unlimited. Media studies, that is, is determined by concepts of media that to a worrisome degree have moved away from the everyday understanding of the medium as a means of communication. This diagnosis is by no means restricted to an isolated current. On the contrary, the inflationary employment of the concept "media," remarkably, can be observed in media theories that understand themselves as competing positions. The technically oriented approach of Marshall McLuhan can document as well as the system-theoretical approach of Niklas Luhmann and the concept of media in phenomenological theories how work is done—if not in the same way, then to the same extent—with an underdetermined concept of media. Just a short look at the main theses of these approaches can show this.

In McLuhan's work media—like all other "technics"—have the status of a means. Media are tools that improve human action and cognition. Just as the hammer is an artificial improvement and expansion of the human body, the McLuhan tradition holds, other media are as well. While mechanical technics relocate the bodily functions of the human being to the exterior, electronic media exterritorialize the central nervous system and the sense organs. Media simulate or amplify, implement or replace bodily and organic capacities. This understanding of media leads McLuhan—and his many followers—to count not only every tool but even every form of energy as part of the meaning of the concept "media." We may sharpen McLuhan's concept of media in the following formulation: the concepts "medium" and "tool" are synonymous.

Niklas Luhmann's system-theoretical concept of media, in particular, deliberately presents itself as an alternative to this technically oriented approach. Luhmann, following Fritz Heider, determines the medium as a possibility for real forms. Media are an open plurality of possible connections. This means that Luhmann and his followers use the concept "medium" with the meaning "opportunity for existence," "disposition," or simply "possibility." Every undetermined possibility that allows for the manifestation of determined forms is a medium. The medium is the opportunity to convert a form into something. That is, completely different from McLuhan's conception, a medium for Luhmann does not itself do anything and is therefore not part of any message either. Media themselves cannot be present and graspable at all, for they are always only a possibility determinable by concrete forms. We may sharpen Luhmann's concept of media in the following formulation: the concepts "medium" and "possibility" become synonymous, and the extension of the concept of media is correspondingly wide; art, society, and the human capacity for perception are all media.

Phenomenological media theories present themselves as yet another alternative—this time both to the technologically oriented and to the system-theoretical approach. This can be observed particularly clearly in Boris Groys's *Unter Verdacht: Eine Phänomenologie der Medien* [Under Suspicion: A Phenomenology of Media].[1] What is particular about phenomenological media theories is that they define media exclusively via their presence with the user of media. For all the differences between phenomenological media theories, one observation is always the focus of interest—the transparency of media or the self-denial of the medium. A medium, accordingly, is a means that functions only when it steps back. To fulfill their function, media must remain unthematized. Put differently, media display something without displaying themselves. In this respect they are comparable to a transparent windowpane that allows for a look outside without itself being seen and through which we only look as long as we do not pay attention to it. Media, from this point of view, do all the more justice to their task the more they neutralize themselves in their employment as media. A well-known description of this medial transparency in Maurice Merleau-Ponty goes as follows:

> Now, one of the effects of language is to efface itself to the extent that its expression comes across. . . . When someone—an author or a friend—succeeds in expressing himself, the signs are immediately forgotten; all that remains is the meaning. The perfection of language lies in its capacity to pass unnoticed.
>
> *But therein lies the virtue of language*: it is language which propels us toward the things its signifies. In the way it works, language hides itself from us. Its triumph is to efface itself.[2]

The consequence of this phenomenological approach is clear. All means that remain unthematized during their employment are addressed as media. Accordingly, signs are media the same way every tool is. Not only is every glove a medium; even one's own body [*Körper*] is explicitly described by Merleau-Ponty as a medium, since it is invisible in the course of perception and action.[3] We have to go even further: there is much to suggest that in the phenomenological tradition the body [*Leib*] is not just an example of a medium but the silent archetype of all media. This, at least, is the conclusion reached by Christian Bermes: "The Body is the Paradigm of Mediality" [Der Leib ist das Paradigma der Medialität]."[4]

To sum up: Even a short look at prominent positions within contemporary media theory shows that the concept of media in each case can hardly be said to correspond to the experience of media, if not in the same way then to the same extent. In all three theoretical approaches the concept of media retains only the most distant connection to the prominent everyday understanding of media as a means of communication. Media theories analyze their own "home-made media," for the phenomena analyzed as media have been identified as such only by the respective theories. We are dealing with media theories of things that without these theories would not be media, such as energy, perception, or the body. In all three cases the concept loses significantly in intension and gains alarmingly in extension.

This progressive de-limitation of the concept of media has by no means gone unnoticed. On the contrary, we might get the impression that in this respect there is a kind of reversal in media studies, especially in the last few years. At least we can observe that the number of critics of concepts of media that are too wide is on the rise. Exemplary of this trend is Matthias Vogel, with his widely noticed study *Medien der Vernunft* [Media of Reason], in which he emphatically warns that in the preeminent media theories, which "are more prone to damaging the reputation of the concept of media in the long run," the "highest point in the process of dedifferentiation" is attained, the point, that is, at which "the concept of media is threatened by substantial erosion."[5]

Georg Christoph Tholen is even more radical in his study *Die Zäsur der Medien* [The Caesura of Media]. He does not even regard the media theories presented above as theoretical contributions but merely cites them as historical examples for the "de-limitation of the figural and authentic meaning" of the concept of media. The classics of media theory, for Tholen, come with a "sprawling metaphorics in the[ir] conceptual attempts at determining the mediality of media." Accordingly they are not interlocutors that are taken seriously systematically but themselves become objects in the investigation of a "metaphorology of media."[6]

In short, what is missing are the differences that make a difference. If with McLuhan every tool, with Luhmann every possibility, and with the phenomenologists every transparency is addressed as medium, there must arise a call for the determination of criteria with which it becomes possible to distinguish the screwdriver from the television set, art from the telephone, and a windowpane from a book. That is why Matthias Vogel is correct in his demands: "An alternative to the turn away from the looming equivocation of media and tools and the devaluation of the concept of media can only come into view if we distinguish the goals to whose actualization media contribute from those that can be achieved with the aid of tools or mere means."[7] This, precisely, seems to be the challenge of a media theory that works systematically: the search for a *differentia specifica* to keep the concept of media from deteriorating into a mere synonym of other concepts. Remarkably, the labor on this question is relevant beyond the concrete problem itself. For as long as media theories work with concepts of media according to which almost anything can be described as a medium, they will be regarded by other disciplines as worrisome academic jacks of all trades, which surely is not conducive to the process of its institutionalization in the academy. If this danger is to be countered by a fruitful perspective, there is no way around advocating a concept of media that has more sense and less meaning, more intension and less extension. And this, precisely, can only be achieved by strictly ensuring that necessary characteristics of media are not treated as sufficient ones.

When we stand on the floor wearing socks and shoes, we usually do not sense our socks and shoes but the floor. We perceive mediately whether we stand or walk on carpet, grass, or concrete. The shoes and socks are not perfectly nonpresent, for it is very well possible to distinguish whether we walk barefoot or in shoes. But this belongs to transparency: it always includes opacity as well. What is decisive, exclusively, is that the shoes and socks are not themselves thematized but that they let the ground below and its properties such as bumps be perceived. And now the crucial question poses itself: how do the socks fare with the media theorist? Only two possible answers are conceivable.

First, the socks and shoes, too, are accepted as media, for after all it is by means of them that a thing that is not directly touched is perceived; they are a transparent extension of the body. Formally speaking, the argument is that transparency is a sufficient phenomenological property of media, which is why all transparent means, that is all tools that are not thematized in their employment, are media.

Second, shoes and socks do indeed have a phenomenal property that media have as well, but this property is not sufficient for media, only necessary. The definition of media via transparency raises a necessary property to the level of a sufficient property. Yet the sufficient property is a completely different one. The same argument can be used for McLuhan and Luhmann. Media are tools but not every tool is a medium, or media offer possibilities but not every possibility is a medium.

If we follow this second path we are concerned with the search for a *differentia specifica*, a sufficient criterion by means of which media can be distinguished from other phenomena that have the same necessary properties. What is remarkable is that what offers itself for this delimitation by means of a sufficient characteristic is a distinction that belongs to the great classical ideas of Husserl's phenomenology. The suggestion is that media are those tools that make it possible to separate genesis from validity. Media, accordingly, are tools or means that are transparent during their employment; but they are also specific tools that are capable of something that other tools cannot achieve, namely a separation of genesis and validity. This suggestion of a definition takes recourse to a genuinely phenomenological idea, albeit an idea that until now has hardly been noticed in phenomenological media theory. This is not surprising insofar as the distinction of genesis and validity was developed by Edmund Husserl at the end of the nineteenth century without any reference whatsoever to media theoretical questions. The separation of genesis and validity that Husserl develops in the first volume of his *Logische Untersuchungen* [*Logical Investigations*] of 1900, following to a large extent similar reflections by Gottlob Frege, is seen as the central argument against psychologism and historism.

Humans are capable of producing something that has no physical properties by means of techniques of production that can be described physically—this is the claim of the separation of genesis and validity. The concept of genesis is used generally for all physical processes. Every process of production or emergence is—in somewhat emphatic terminology, to be sure—addressed as "genesis." Put tautologically, this means that genesis is the genetic process that generates something. These processes take place in space and time; they are empirical facts and can accordingly be studied with the means of different empirical sciences. Thus, for example, it can always be determined when such a process of emergence begins and when it ends, where it takes place and under which conditions it unfolds. An empirical process is always a process that can be changed and also be destroyed, that is to say aborted—and this is not the case for validities. We can speak of a validity when something seems to exist that has no physical properties. Indeed, it is easiest to determine validity negatively, by saying what it is not: it is something that is not physically graspable yet to which humans can nonetheless refer. We sense this nonphysicality of validities in particular when we take notice of time. Every empirical thing is subject to time; it becomes older and changes in time. If something is unchangeable and does not become older, then it cannot be an empirical thing. What is in the world also ages with the world. In considering time, Husserl describes the decisive difference between empirical processes and validities. Validities are "untouched by the contingency, temporality and transience of our mental acts."[8] His example is a mathematical calculation. If we take the proposition 2 x 2 = 4, then we have on the one hand an empirical speech act, a materialized process in space and time, a physically describable phenomenon. Yet on the other hand we also have the validity of this proposition, which is not dependent on who formulates this proposition when and how: "Acts of counting arise and pass away and cannot be meaningfully mentioned in the same breath as numbers."[9] What Husserl means is a difference that is as simple as it is important: if the proposition 2 x 2 = 4 is printed in a book, this material sentence will age, yellow; it can be erased, or the book can be destroyed. But what is meant by the proposition is not touched by these changes in time; the content of the proposition does not grow older, which is why Husserl writes, "In this sphere there can be no talk of individual facts, of what is temporally definite."[10] Hence a property is present that cannot be thought physically: everything that has a physical existence must grow older. Yet validities are removed from the ravages of time because they are not physically existent. What is not in time cannot be changed by physical force. Husserl writes, therefore, "My act of judging that 2 x 2 = 4 is no doubt causally determined, but this is not true of the truth 2 x 2 = 4."[11]

Husserl's example has one great disadvantage: it suggests that truth and validity are identical. Yet this precisely is not the case. What this is about is just that different people at different times can mean the same thing by the proposition 2 x 2 = 4. Validity is a precondition equally for truth and for falsity. For even someone who wants to claim that the proposition 2 x 2 = 4 is by no means always true finds him- or herself in opposition to whoever thinks, like Husserl, that the proposition 2 x 2 = 4 is always true only if both mean the same thing by their different propositions and thus are of a different opinion about the same thing. Only if we are of different opinions about the same thing are we of different opinions—and this, precisely, is what validity is: the existence of something that is the same for several people at different times.

In light of the classic distinction of genesis and validity the question imposes itself: how is this possible? How can something that does not have any physical properties be generated with physical tools? The question seems unanswerable because in the end it asks how thinking and rationality are possible. Yet even if we cannot explain how something is possible, we can sometimes describe what is necessary for it, in this case: media. Media are necessary for the separation of genesis and validity—other tools are incapable of this, which is why the following definition imposes itself: media are precisely those tools with which this separation can miraculously be accomplished and which constitute at the same time the mediation between both moments. "Separation" here does not mean that one could, so to speak, really isolate validity and cut it off from the hardware and put it aside like a thing. "Separation" means that media always consist of a genesis aspect and a validity aspect and that this conceptual distinction is necessary and possible in their case alone. Husserl's example already shows this: only somebody who employs a conceptual language as a medium is capable of thinking by means of the proposition 2 x 2 = 4 something that can also be thought by other people at other times by means of this medium. Human beings can think things and relations that do not grow older, that cannot be influenced by physical processes, only with the help of the medium language. In short, only by means of media can different human beings at different times think and mean not only something equivalent but also the very same thing [*nicht nur das gleiche, sondern dasselbe*].[12] We may even determine the somewhat antiquated concept "validity" as follows: validity is artificial self-sameness [*Selbigkeit*], and media are the means for the production of artificial self-sameness.

In many books, in many locations, the self-same novel can be read—it is precisely this self-same novel that affects so many people so differently, that is at different times interpreted and understood so differently. Hardly anyone would seriously want to claim that only those have read the same novel who really held the self-same copy in their hands. Everybody who has read Thomas Mann's *The Magic Mountain* has not read a merely equivalent, but the very same, novel. Husserl writes about his example, the proposition 2 x 2 = 4, that this judgment "is the same whoever passes it."[13] Following this formulation we could say that the novel *The Magic Mountain* is always the very same novel, no matter who prints it. The movie *The Matrix* is always the very same movie, no matter when and where it is watched. A home page is always the very same home page, no matter with which computer and on what screen it may be generated. In this way the fundamental capacity of media becomes determinable: media allow for the production, in different places and at different times, not only of an equivalent but also of the very same thing. And because everybody can at different times and in different places read the very same novel, make the very same judgment, and see the very same image, it can no longer be said that what, thanks to media, comes about as validity is a private affair. Medial validity exists only in communal form: "The number five is not my own."[14] Of course there are the private psychological acts of thinking with which someone at a specific moment thinks the number five but because of the employment of a medium—namely conceptual language—the very same thing that this person thinks in this moment can also be thought by another person at another moment. There is of course the private copy of Mann's *The Magic Mountain*, that is, the unique kind of genesis of the novel that sits on a bookshelf in someone's home. Yet the content of the book can no more be private property than the number five—for content does not exist as a physical something but as a validity. The parallel to Husserl, therefore, is the following: just as writing is a medium by means of which many people can read the very same novel, so language is a medium by means of which many people can think the very same number.

These reflections show us what is meant by such widespread concepts as "storage media" and "distribution media." If media as a whole are the means by which human beings can perceive and think something that has no physical properties, then this validity is stored in storage media and distributed in distribution media. It is quite inapt to call every means of storage and every means of transportation a medium. Storage media, to be more precise, are media for the storage of validities, and distribution media are media for the distribution of validities, for the simple reason that what a storage medium stores is something special: something that does not grow older. The grain of wheat that is stored in a granary is subject to the laws of physics. No refrigerator, no matter how good, will ever be a storage medium because no matter how well it preserves the food stored within, it will not suspend the laws of physics. That is why storage media are not optimized refrigerators. A symphony that is stored in a score or on a CD no longer changes. In this sense distribution media do not allow for the distribution of just anything but for the distribution of self-sameness. Many people in many places can nonetheless see the very same TV program. No transport company has this capacity. The very same thing can be present in different places and at different times only through media.

It seems to be a genuinely phenomenological concern to pursue the idea that media produce and allow for something whose specific qualities can be described; media can be recognized by the phenomenological properties of their products. The particularity of this approach becomes clear when we compare it to the definition proposed by Lorenz Engell and Joseph Vogl in the preface to their ambitious collection *Kursbuch Medienkultur: Die maßgeblichen Theorien von Brecht bis Baudrillard* [A Guide to Media Culture: The Authoritative Theories from Brecht to Baudrillard], which reads: "Media make legible, audible, visible, perceivable, yet all of this with the tendency to erase themselves and their constitutive participation in these sensibilities and thus to become as if imperceptible, anaesthetic."[15] To be sure, hardly anyone would want to contradict the claim that media make legible, audible, and visible. Yet when we reduce media to this capacity, we implicitly claim that what is made legible, audible, or visible by media is not distinct from what is legible, audible, or visible without media. The use of media, so to speak, would have no effect on what is made visible with them. Yet it is here, precisely, that a phenomenological description can pick up: what is made visible by media is of a fundamentally different kind than what is visible without a medium. We can tell that what was made visible by a medium was made visible that way: media make visible, audible, legible something that does not exist physically. That is why we are not dealing with a medial process when something physically existing is made visible. When the light is turned on in the basement, it makes the things stored there visible—but the light is not a medium; it only lets things become visible that behave according to the laws of physics. The same is true for mirrors. In the case of media it is exactly the other way around: they exclusively make things visible that would not be capable of being visible without media because they are nonphysical things. This does not in the least mean that media are remarkable and relevant only with respect to this specific capacity of theirs. On the contrary, very often it would be a distorting reduction to concentrate, in medial processes, only on the validity and not on the materiality of the medium employed. In quite a few aesthetic contexts it even is the materiality of the media employed that is of preeminent significance. Nonetheless, no material property explains why something is a medium. Only certain materials and technologies are addressed as media, namely those with which self-sameness can be produced. This difference can be depicted particularly well in the case of images.

The visibility of the image is, medially conditioned, a kind of visibility that is fundamentally different from that of a real thing. For the image object visible on an image carrier is distinct both from the material that makes visible and, as the case may be, from the denotatum symbolized by the image object. The image object is visible, but it has properties that a real visible thing cannot have, which is why we hardly confuse an image object with a real thing: it does not grow older; it cannot have light shed on it; it cannot be touched; it cannot be examined under a microscope; it cannot move; it cannot trigger any physical effects; and it cannot be looked at from the side. That is why two moviegoers, even though one may be sitting all the way to the left and the other all the way to the right in the movie theater, still see the very same film, even if they do not look at the screen from the same direction. (This, by the way, is not true for theater; there, it may very well be the case that not everything on the stage can be seen from every place in the audience.) What is seen in an image are autonomous things that are perfectly taken out of physical reality, things that are not part of the world. It is as if Hans Jonas wanted to hint at the characteristics of validity when he writes in his essay "Homo pictor and the Differentia of Man" that the world visible in the image is "removed from the causal commerce of things."[16] In short, the image object has no physical existence but is nothing other than the visible validity of an image. This certainly surprising consequence indeed seems inevitable. What Husserl calls image object is only a form of appearance of visible validity specific to the medium of the image. This interpretation and, in particular, the formulation "visible validity" seem unusual only as long as the problematic of validity is discussed in reference to problems of mathematics and propositional truth alone. Yet in Husserl himself we do not find this limitation. In a small, somewhat hidden short remark that he makes in a supplement to the fifth of the *Logical Investigations* he explicitly clarifies that image objects are perceived validities: "The painting is only an image for an image-constituting consciousness, that is a consciousness that by means of its imaginative apperception endows a primary object that appears to it perceptually with the 'validity' or 'meaning' of an image in the first place."[17] This makes it clear that validity in the case of the image is an object that is perceived and that is no longer subject to the laws of physics, and that media are the tools that must be employed for the separation of genesis and validity. Media make legible, audible, and visible—but something special becomes legible, audible, and visible through them: namely intersubjective self-sameness, that is, validity. That is why we can say that media are precisely those tools that make it possible that not just something *equivalent* but also the *very same thing* can be seen, heard, and thought at different times, in different places, by different people—and this likely is the reason why media can hardly be overestimated in their anthropological significance.

If humans had no media, they would be a mere piece of the world—like jellyfish, they would stand in a relation of identity to their environment, if in that case we can even speak of environment. Humans are part of the world—but precisely not just that, since by means of media they participate in realities that do not behave like the world of physical things. If humans had no media, they could only see what is present; they could only see what they could also hear, smell, and touch. Only because there are media are humans capable of seeing, hearing, and thinking the very same content at two different points in time. Nature does not know of the self-same, only of the equivalent. The camera is a visibility isolation machine: it separates visibility from the present physical substance of a thing. Yet what is not physically there, like an image object, has no physics; it is fantastically nonphysical. That is why images can display matters of fact that are physically impossible. Precisely this, the ability to think and perceive physical impossibilities, is possible only with media; they are the only means humans have to disempower physics. That is why without media no human existence that is more than the presence of stuff can emerge. Because there are media, humans live not only in physical nature but also in a culture, and they therefore owe their human existence to the employment of media. Thus results a perspective for work on media that is as phenomenological as it is anthropological: media liberate humans from the ubiquitously present dictates of the physical world.

Notes

CHAPTER 2

This chapter is a significantly revised version of "Medienphilosophie des Bildes" [Media Philosophy of the Image], *Deutsche Zeitschrift für Philosophie* 7 (2004): 147–62.

1. Until now, classifications usually reduce currents in the philosophy of the image to two: a semiotic (or analytical) current and a current based on perception (or phenomenological current). See, for example, Klaus Sachs-Hombach, *Bildbegriff und Bildwissenschaft* [Concept of the Image and Image Studies] (Saarbrücken: Galerie St. Johann, 2001), 16–18; and Oliver R. Scholz, "Bild" [Image], in *Ästhetische Grundbegriffe*, ed. Karlheinz Barck, Martin Fontius, and Dieter Schlenstedt, vol. 1 (Stuttgart: Metzler, 2000), 618–69, 667–69.

2. Hans Jonas, "Homo pictor and the Differentia of Man," *Social Research* 29, no. 2 (summer 1962): 201–20, 212. [This text, as Jonas points out in a note on p. 201, formed the basis for Jonas's own German translation, which "got into print before the original" in 1961; this translation, included in the collection *Zwischen Nichts und Ewigkeit: Drei Aufsätze zur Lehre vom Menschen* (Göttingen: Vandenhoek und Ruprecht, 1963), 26–43, is the text Lambert Wiesing has used.—Trans.]

3. Jonas, "Homo pictor and the Differentia of Man," 210.

4. Ibid., 217.

5. [The sentence this quote is taken from was not included by Jonas in the published English version, where it would have found its place on p. 218, in the discussion of the determination of the body by the will. In the German text it can be found on p. 40.—Trans.]

6. Jonas, "Homo pictor and the Differentia of Man," 215.

7. Vilém Flusser, "Eine neue Einbildungskraft" [A New Power of the Imagination], in *Bildlichkeit*, ed. Volker Bohn (Frankfurt: Suhrkamp, 1990), 115–26, 115–16.

8. Jean-Paul Sartre, *The Imaginary: A Phenomenological Psychology of the Imagination*, rev. Arlette Elkaïm-Sartre, trans. Jonathan Webber (London: Routledge, 2004), 179–88.

9. Hans Belting, *Bild-Anthropologie: Entwürfe für eine Bildwissenschaft* [Anthropology of the Image: Sketches for Image Studies] (Munich: Fink, 2001), dust jacket.

10. Ibid., 20.

11. Ibid.

12. Ibid., 213.

13. Ibid., 57.

14. Ibid., 65.

15. Tilman Reitz, "Der Mensch im Bild: Konservative Alternativen zur Kunstgeschichte," *Philosophische Rundschau* 50 (2003): 170–78, 173; the quotations are from Belting, *Bild-Anthropologie*, 75.

16. Belting, *Bild-Anthropologie*, 23.

17. Reitz, "Der Mensch im Bild," 173.

18. Belting, *Bild-Anthropologie*, 185–86.

19. Georges Didi-Huberman, *Ce que nous voyons, ce qui nous regarde* (Paris: Minuit, 1992), 14.

20. Nelson Goodman, *Languages of Art: An Approach to a Theory of Symbols* (Indianapolis: Hackett, 1976), xi.

21. Ibid., 5.

22. For a discussion of resemblance in analytic image theories see Klaus Rehkämper, *Bilder, Ähnlichkeit und Perspektive: Auf dem Weg zu einer neuen Theorie der bildhaften Repräsentation* [Images, Resemblance, and Perspective: On the Path to a New Theory of Pictorial Representation] (Wiesbaden: DUV, 2002).

23. Jonas, "Homo pictor and the Differentia of Man," 207. [Jonas renders "das Dargestellte, die Darstellung und das Darstellende" as "the represented, the representation, and the vehicle of representation." As I translate *Darstellung* throughout as "depiction," I have rendered the same phrase as "the depicted, the depiction, and the depicting" a few lines down.—Trans.]

24. Ibid.

25. Sachs-Hombach, *Bildbegriff und Bildwissenschaft*, 18.

26. It is no surprise that from this fundamental orientation, the concern to develop an alternative to the semiotic description and the linguification of the image, there should result a communality of the anthropological and perception-based approaches; Hans Belting understands himself to be an "anti-semiotician" (Hans Belting, "Das Bild als anthropologisches Phänomen" [The Image as an Anthropological Phenomenon], in *Wege zur Bildwissenschaft*, ed. Klaus Sachs-Hombach [Cologne: von Halem, 2004], 116–26, 120).

27. Edmund Husserl, *Logical Investigations*, trans. J. N. Findlay, ed. Dermot Moran (London: Routledge, 2001), pt. 1, 5th Investigation, supplement to §§ 11 and 20, 126 [modified].

28. Jean-Paul Sartre, "What Is Literature?" (1948) trans. Bernard Frechtman, in *"What Is Literature?" and Other Essays* (Cambridge, MA: Harvard University Press, 1988), 21–245, 26–27 [modified].

29. Konrad Fiedler, *Vom Ursprung der künstlerischen Tätigkeit* [On the Origin of Artistic Activity] (1887), in *Schriften zur Kunst*, vol. 2, ed. Gottfried Boehm (Munich: Fink, 1991), 192.

30. Ibid., 191.

31. Ibid., 192.

32. Sartre's term is *désincarné*; cf. Jean-Paul Sartre, "Portraits officiels," in *Visages; précédé de Portraits officiels* (Paris: Seghers, 1948), 11–18, 16 ["Official Portraits," trans. Anne P. Jones, in *Essays in Phenomenology*, ed. Maurice Natanson (The Hague: Nijhoff, 1966), 157–58, 158].

33. Fiedler, *Vom Ursprung der künstlerischen Tätigkeit*, 191, 161.

34. See Fritz Heider, "Ding und Medium" [Thing and Medium], *Symposium* 2 (1926): 109–57, 119.

35. Sachs-Hombach, *Bildbegriff und Bildwissenschaft*, 18.

36. Goodman, *Languages of Art*, 14.

37. Ibid., 5.

38. Husserl, *Logical Investigations*, pt. 1, 5th Investigation, supplement to §§ 11 and 20, 125 [modified].

39. Hans Ulrich Gumbrecht, *Production of Presence: What Meaning Cannot Convey* (Stanford, CA: Stanford University Press, 2004), 78.

40. Ibid., 16.

CHAPTER 3

1. Max Bense, *Semiotik: Allgemeine Theorie der Zeichen* [Semiotics: General Theory of Signs] (Baden-Baden: Agis, 1967), 9.

2. Max Bense, *Aesthetica: Einführung in die neue Aesthetik* [Aesthetica: Introduction to the New Aesthetics] (Baden-Baden: Agis, 1965), 305.

3. Ibid.

4. Charles Sanders Peirce, *Elements of Logic*, vol. 2 of *Collected Papers*, ed. Charles Hartshorne and Paul Weiss (Cambridge, MA: Harvard University Press, 1932), 308.

5. Ludwig Wittgenstein, *Philosophical Investigations*, trans. G. E. M. Anscombe, 2nd ed. (Oxford: Blackwell, 1958), pt. 1, prop. 432, p. 128.

6. Charles Sanders Peirce, "On the Nature of Signs," in *Writings of Charles S. Peirce: A Chronological Edition*, vol. 3, ed. Christian J. W. Kloesel (Bloomington: Indiana University Press, 1986), 66–68, 66.

7. Reinhard Brandt, *Die Wirklichkeit des Bildes* [The Actuality of the Image] (Munich: Hanser, 1999), 132.

8. Winfried Nöth, "Zeichentheoretische Grundlagen der Bildwissenschaft" [Semiotic Foundations of Image Studies], in *Bildwissenschaft zwischen Reflexion und Anwendung*, ed. Klaus Sachs-Hombach (Cologne: von Halem, 2004), 33–44, 33.

9. Ibid.

10. Ibid., 33, 38.

11. Roland Posner and Dagmar Schmauks, "Die Reflektiertheit der Dinge und ihre Darstellung in Bildern," in *Bild—Bildwahrnehmung—Bildverarbeitung: Interdisziplinäre Beiträge zur Bildwissenschaft*, ed. Klaus Sachs-Hombach and Klaus Rehkämper (Wiesbaden: DUV, 1998), 15–33, 15.

12. Nöth, "Zeichentheoretische Grundlagen der Bildwissenschaft," 33.

13. Ibid.

14. Klaus Sachs-Hombach, *Das Bild als kommunikatives Medium: Elemente einer allgemeinen Bildwissenschaft* [The Image as Communicative Medium: Elements of General Image Studies] (Cologne: von Halem, 2003), 77.

15. Whether this usage still follows Ferdinand de Saussure's original intention seems to be an interpretational issue. It is hardly a matter of dispute, however, that this usage has established itself. Umberto Eco, too, sees that "in philosophical discourse, 'sign' is almost always used as a synonym of 'signifier,' i.e., it is used as 'something that stands for something else'" (Umberto Eco, *Il Segno*, Enciclopedia filosofica ISEDI 2 [Milan: Istituto Editoriale Internazionale, 1973], 27).

16. Goodman, *Languages of Art*, 5.

17. Edmund Husserl, "Phantasy and Image Consciousness," in *Phantasy, Image Consciousness, and Memory (1898–1925)*, trans. John B. Brough (Dordrecht: Springer, 2005), § 9.21.

18. Ibid., § 39.88.

19. Ibid., § 8.20 [modified].

20. Klaus Rehkämper, *Bilder, Ähnlichkeit und Perspektive: Auf dem Weg zu einer neuen Theorie der bildhaften Repräsentation* [Images, Resemblance, and Perspective: On the Path to a New Theory of Pictorial Representation] (Wiesbaden: DUV, 2002), 110.

21. Roland Barthes, *Elements of Semiology* (New York: Hill and Wang, 1968), 2.3.1.47 [modified].

22. Goodman, *Languages of Art*, 5.

23. Ibid., 50.

24. Sachs-Hombach, *Das Bild als kommunikatives Medium*, 73–99.

25. Peirce, *Elements of Logic*, 247.

26. Goodman, *Languages of Art*, 41–42.

27. Ibid., 42.

28. Husserl, "Phantasy and Image Consciousness," § 9.20.

29. Ibid., § 9.21.

30. Ibid., § 9.22.

31. Husserl, *Logical Investigations*, pt. 1, 5th Investigation, supplement to §§ 11 and 20, 126 [modified].

32. E. H. Gombrich, "Experiment and Experience in the Arts" (1980), in *The Image and the Eye: Further Studies in the Psychology of Pictorial Representation* (Oxford: Phaidon, 1982), 215–43, 228.

33. E. H. Gombrich, "Mirror and Map: Theories of Pictorial Representation" (1974), in *The Image and the Eye*, 172–214, 194.

34. Husserl, "Phantasy and Image Consciousness," § 38.86.

35. Ibid., § 14.30.

36. Husserl, *Logical Investigations*, pt. 1, 5th Investigation, supplement to §§ 11 and 20, 126 [modified].

37. Ibid.

38. Goodman, *Languages of Art*, 41.

39. Resemblance is a partial identity. In the case of images this identity concerns visible properties and visible *Gestalt* phenomena [*Gestaltphänomene*]. The image object is an object that—like any other object—can have the same visible properties and *Gestalten* partially and in degrees as any other visible object. When we look at an image carrier and believe we see something that has blond hair, we see an image object that has the same property as do real human beings with blond hair. In short, image objects and real things have common properties, and if this partial identity in terms of visible properties becomes as such a conscious one, there exists for a viewer a resemblance between these two objects. This resemblance also concerns common visible relations, arrangements, shapes, and forms. Without a doubt the most important form for the description of pictorial resemblance, as Klaus Rehkämper has convincingly argued, is the so-called P-form, which is always that common property of an image object (an image object constructed according to a central perspective) and precisely that real thing for which this image object can be used as a pictorial sign. Rehkämper defines the P-form as follows: "The P-form of an object is the two-dimensional central projection of this object relative to an observer's point of view, a vision cone [*Sehkegel*] and a plumb image surface. The P-form of an object O is an objective property of O. Nonetheless, an object possesses several P-forms relative to several points of view and vision cones. A perspectival image displays a P-form of its denotatum" (Rehkämper, *Bilder, Ähnlichkeit und Perspektive*, 5). Yet this does not at all mean that the mere display of a P-form automatically turns the image—of its own, so to say—into a symbolic representation of that object whose P-form is displayed. The P-form that is visibly present can be used as a pictorial sign for precisely those real objects that have this displayed P-form as a visible property. Yet this use, which is contingent and conventional, must accompany the display of a P-form in order for a nonconventional, mathematically governed relation between an image object constructed

according to a central perspective and a real thing to become a relation of reference from the image object to the real thing. Display by itself is not a reference.

40. Hilary Putnam, *Reason, Truth and History* (Cambridge, UK: Cambridge University Press, 1981), 1.

41. Just as an imitation does not have to be an image: the concept of imitation encompasses depictions as well as copies or replicas [*Imitationen*] that are not images. Chapter 7 describes this differentiation and its gradual emergence in Plato.

42. Husserl, "Phantasy and Image Consciousness," § 17.40 [modified].

43. Goodman, *Languages of Art*, 26.

44. Chapter 4 will try to describe more closely the concept of the photograph and its complicated relation to the concept of the image.

45. Nöth, "Zeichentheoretische Grundlagen der Bildwissenschaft," 35.

46. Dieter Mersch, *Was sich zeigt: Materialität, Präsenz, Ereignis* [What Shows Itself: Materiality, Presence, Event] (Munich: Fink, 2002), 11.

47. Husserl, "Phantasy and Image Consciousness," § 11.24 [modified].

48. Ibid., § 11.24–25.

49. Ibid., § 14.32.

50. Ibid., § 13.29.

51. Ibid., § 39.88.

52. Ibid., § 17.40 [modified].

53. Ibid. § 32.74.

54. Ibid., § 17.39 [modified].

55. Goodman, *Languages of Art*, 52.

56. Husserl, "Phantasy and Image Consciousness," § 12.26 [modified].

57. Hippolyte Taine, *On Intelligence*, trans. T. D. Haye (London: Reeve, 1871), 52. Even before Husserl, as this quote shows, Hippolyte Taine clearly depicted the decisive idea that image consciousness is based on an antagonism of two perceptions. On this point see also Lambert Wiesing, *Phänomene im Bild* [Phenomena in the Image] (Munich: Fink, 2007), 51–54.

58. Goodman, *Languages of Art*, 86.

59. Sartre, "What Is Literature?" 27.

CHAPTER 4

This chapter is an abbreviated version of the essay "Abstrakte Fotographie Denk-und Bildmöglichkeiten," in the bilingual volume *Abstrakte Fotografie/Abstract Photography*, by Lambert Wiesing and Gottfried Jäger (Bielefeld: Teutloff, 2000), retranslated for the present volume.

1. See Alvin Langdon Coburn, "The Future of Pictorial Photography," *Photograms of the Year* (1916), 23–24.

2. Answers to the question *What is abstract photography?* relevant in this context can be found in Gottfried Jäger, *Bildgebende Fotografie: Fotografik—Lichtgrafik—Lichtmalerei: Ursprünge, Konzepte und Spezifika einer Kunstform* [Image-Giving Photography: Photographics—Light Graphics—Light Painting: Origins, Concepts and Specifics of a Form of Art] (Cologne: DuMont, 1988); Floris M. Neusüss, *Das Fotogramm in der Kunst des 20. Jahrhunderts: Die andere Seite der Bilder—Fotografie ohne Kamera* [The Photogram in Twentieth-Century Art: The Other Side of Images—Photography without a Camera] (Cologne: DuMont, 1990); and Gottfried Jäger, "Die Kunst der Abstrakten Fotografie," in *Die Kunst der Abstrakten Fotografie / The Art of Abstract Photography*, ed. Gottfried Jäger (Stuttgart: Arnoldsche, 2002), 11–72.

3. Gottfried Jäger, "Abbildungstreue: Fotografie als Visualisierung: Zwischen Bilderfahrung und Bilderfindung" [Fidelity in Picturing: Photography as Visualization: Between Pictorial Experience and Pictorial Invention], in *Visualisierung in Mathematik, Technik und Kunst*, ed. Andreas Dress and Gottfried Jäger (Braunschweig and Wiesbaden: Vieweg, 1999), 137–50, 145.

4. Roman Ingarden, "The Picture," in *Ontology of the Work of Art* (1931), trans. Raymond Meyer with John T. Goldthwait (Athens: Ohio University Press, 1989), 135–251, § 9.214 [modified].

5. Jäger, "Abbildungstreue," 142.

6. Gottfried Jäger, "Nicht eine Vorstellung realisieren, sondern eine Realität vorstellen, das ist: Fotografie," in *Fotoästhetik: Zur Theorie der Fotografie* [Photo Aesthetics: On the Theory of Photography] (Munich: Laterna Magica, 1991), 13. On the concept of generative photography see also Gottfried Jäger and Karl Martin Holzhäuser, *Generative Fotografie: Theoretische Grundlegung, Kompendium und Beispiele einer fotografischen Bildgestaltung* [Generative Photography: Theoretical Foundation, Compendium, and Examples of Photographic Pictorial Design] (Ravensburg: Maier, 1975).

CHAPTER 5

This chapter is a significantly revised version of "Fenster, Fernseher und Windows," *Journal Phänomenologie* 15 (2001): 15–19.

1. Leon Batista Alberti, *On Painting*, trans. John R. Spencer (New Haven, CT: Yale University Press, 1966), 56 [modified].

2. Jean-Paul Sartre, "What Is Literature?" trans. Bernard Frechtman, in *"What Is Literature?" and Other Essays* (Cambridge, MA: Harvard University Press, 1988), 63.

3. Edmund Husserl, "Phantasy and Image Consciousness," in *Phantasy, Image Consciousness, and Memory (1898–1925)*, trans. John B. Brough (Dordrecht: Springer, 2005), § 22.50 [modified].

4. Ibid., § 14.33.

5. Ibid., § 26.59 [modified].

6. Ibid., § 14.35.

7. [The German for TV set, *Fernseher*, literally means "far-looker"; *television, Fernsehen*, is "seeing far."—Trans.]

8. See the facsimile of the patent in Heide Riedel, *Fernsehen—Von der Vision zum Programm: 50 Jahre Programmdienst in Deutschland* [Television—From Vision to Program: Fifty Years of Program Service in Germany] (Berlin: Deutsches Rundfunk-Museum, 1985), 20–23.

9. Wilhelm and Jacob Grimm, eds., *The Complete Fairy Tales*, trans. Ralph Manheim (New York: Doubleday, 1990), 202–5, 202.

10. Quoted in Heinz Brüggemann, *Das andere Fenster: Einblicke in Häuser und Menschen: Zur Literaturgeschichte einer urbanen Wahrnehmungsform* [The Other Window: Insights into Houses and Humans: On the Literary History of an Urban Form of Perception] (Frankfurt: Fischer, 1989), 300.

11. [In the original German: "Kurt Schwitters würde sagen: Düsseldorf ist auch kein Dorf." *Dorf* means village and forms part of the name of many towns and cities, such as Düsseldorf, a state capital with hundreds of thousands of inhabitants.—Trans.]

12. [The term *Schaufenster*, here translated in its common meaning as "shop window," includes *schauen*, "to look"; this added dimension lets it be employed in the sense of a window that is made for things to be looked at in general, not just for marketing purposes.—Trans.]

13. Cf. Axel Müller, "Albertis Fenster: Gestaltwandel einer ikonischen Metapher" [Alberti's Window: Transformations in an Iconic Metaphor's Figure], in *Bild—Bildwahrnehmung—Bildverarbeitung: Interdisziplinäre Beiträge zur Bildwissenschaft*, ed. Klaus Sachs-Hombach and Klaus Rehkämper (Wiesbaden: DUV, 1998), 173–83.

14. Herbert W. Franke, "Der Monitor als Fenster in einen unbegrenzten Raum" [The Computer Screen as a Window onto an Unlimited Space], in *Digitaler Schein: Ästhetik der elektronischen Medien*, ed. Florian Rötzer (Frankfurt: Suhrkamp, 1991), 282–93, 283.

15. Ibid.

CHAPTER 6

This chapter is based on the author's November 2001 Inaugural Lecture at the Friedrich Schiller University, Jena.

1. Oliver Grau, *Virtual Art: From Illusion to Immersion*, trans. Gloria Custance (Cambridge, MA: MIT Press, 2003), 15.

2. Ibid., 7.

3. Jean-Paul Sartre, *The Imaginary: A Phenomenological Psychology of the Imagination*, rev. Arlette Elkaïm-Sartre, trans. Jonathan Webber (London: Routledge, 2004), 12.

4. Edmund Husserl, "Phantasy and Image Consciousness," in *Phantasy, Image Consciousness, and Memory (1898–1925)*, trans. John B. Brough (Dordrecht: Springer, 2005), § 29.65.

5. Ibid., § 28.65 [modified].

6. We find the attempt to differentiate the mode of givenness of changes in the contents of fantasy from the mode of givenness of changes in film in Husserl as well. He points out explicitly that "the alteration in the image, which normally can be confirmed during a phantasy presentation that does not last for too short a time absolutely must not be confused with changes in the appearance that moves within the synthesis of the nexus of appearances" ("Phantasy and Image Consciousness," § 29.67 [modified]). For Husserl, however, the difference between film and fantasy does not consist in the exactly repeatable determinedness of the changes in film but in that the changes in film are tied to the unity of the image object or of the image subject: "Even if the image is one that moves, as in the stroboscope, say, or in the motion picture, the unity of the presenting and, correspondingly, of the representational nexus (to which the unity of the object unfolding in it corresponds) is preserved" (ibid., § 29.66 [modified]).

7. Vilém Flusser, *Ins Universum der technischen Bilder* [Into the Universe of Technical Images], 4th ed. (Göttingen: European Photography, 1992), 42.

8. Vilém Flusser, "Eine neue Einbildungskraft" [A New Power of the Imagination], in *Bildlichkeit*, ed. Volker Bohn (Frankfurt: Suhrkamp, 1990), 115–26, 123.

9. Jaron Lanier, "Life in the Data-Cloud," *Mondo 2000*, no. 2 (1990): 44–54, 46.

10. Sartre, *The Imaginary*, 11 [modified; the emphasis is Sartre's].

11. Flusser, "Eine neue Einbildungskraft," 123–24.

12. On this question see Frank Stäudner, "Virtuelle Erfahrung: Eine Untersuchung über den Erkenntniswert von Gedankenexperimenten und Computersimulationen in den Naturwissenschaften" [Virtual Experience: A Study on the Epistemological Value of Thought Experiments and Computer Simulations in the Natural Sciences] (PhD diss., Universität Jena, 1998).

13. Flusser, *Ins Universum der technischen Bilder*, 43.

CHAPTER 7

This chapter is a slightly revised version of "Platons Mimesis-Begriff und sein verborgener Kanon," in *Begründungen und Funktionen des Kanons: Beiträge aus der Literatur- und Kunstwissenschaft, Philosophie und Theologie*, ed. Gerhard R. Kaiser and Stefan Matuschek (Heidelberg: Winter, 2001), 21–41.

1. See Karl Raimund Popper, *The Spell of Plato*, vol. 1 of *The Open Society and Its Enemies* (London: Routledge, 1945).

2. Plato, *Republic*, trans. G. M. A. Grube, rev. C. D. C. Reeve, *Complete Works*, ed. John M. Cooper and D. S. Hutchinson (Indianapolis: Hackett, 1997), 971–1223, 599a–b [modified]. [As the question of translation is central to Wiesing's discussion, the quotes from Plato that follow are taken from Cooper and Hutchinson's edition but modified in light of Schleiermacher's translation (Platon, *Der Staat*, vol. 4 of *Werke in acht Bänden*, trans. Friedrich Schleiermacher, ed. Gunther Eigler [Darmstadt: Wissenschaftliche Buchgesellschaft, 1990]), which remains the canonical rendering, shaping like none other the interpretation of Plato in Germany.—Trans.]

3. Plato, *Republic*, 598c–e, 601c–602b.

4. Andreas Schubert, *Platon, "Der Staat": Ein einführender Kommentar* [Plato, "The Republic": An Introductory Commentary] (Paderborn: Schöningh, 1995), 161.

5. Plato, *Republic*, 600e.

6. Ibid., 602d.

7. Ibid., 595c. [The English edition used here has "imitation."—Trans.]

8. Maria Kardaun gives a good overview of the translations of *mimesis* proposed thus far, as well as a helpful discussion of what translation of this vague and broad concept is at what point appropriate, in *Der Mimesis-Begriff in der griechischen Antike: Neubetrachtung eines umstrittenen Begriffs als Ansatz zu einer neuen Interpretation der platonischen Kunstauffassung* [The Concept of Mimesis in Greek Antiquity: A New Look at a Controversial Concept as Point of Departure for a New Interpretation of Plato's Conception of Art] (Amsterdam: North-Holland, 1993).

9. On this point see also Karlheinz Lüdeking, "Zwischen den Linien: Vermutungen zum aktuellen Frontverlauf im Bilderstreit" [Between the Lines: Conjectures on the Current Front Lines in the Image Controversy], in *Was ist ein Bild?* ed. Gottfried Boehm (Munich: Fink, 1994), 344–66.

10. On this point see Hans Belting, *Likeness and Presence: A History of the Image Before the Era of Art*, trans. Edmund Jephcott (Chicago: University of Chicago Press, 1993).

11. Plato, *Republic,* 420c–d.

12. This difference between painting and sculpture must be heeded especially when what is to be determined are the concealed canonic work conceptions of the Old Testament's prohibition of images. For here, as Reinhard Hoeps has been able to show, we have the remarkable case that the opposition against images really refers to sculptures and plastic art: "The criticism and polemics of the Old Testament do not conceptualize their ideas of pictoriality against the image of God in terms of sculpture and plastic art, but it is from there that they draw their guiding intuitions" (Reinhard Hoeps, *Aus dem Schatten des goldenen Kalbes: Skulptur in theologischer Perspektive* [Out of the Shadow of the Golden Calf: Sculpture in Theological Perspective] [Paderborn: Schöningh, 1999], 20).

13. On the ancient concept of stage painting see Nadia J. Koch, *Techne und Erfindung in der klassischen Malerei: Eine terminologische Untersuchung* [Tekhnē and Invention in Classical Painting: A Terminological Study] (Munich: Biering und Brinkmann, 2000), 83–90.

14. Plato, *Sophist*, trans. Nicholas P. White, *Complete Works*, ed. John M. Cooper and D. S. Hutchinson (Indianapolis: Hackett, 1997), 235–93, 235b–236d. [Once again, the English will be revised in light of Schleiermacher's translation into German, in Platon, *Werke in acht Bänden*, ed. Gunther Eigler, vol. 6 (Darmstadt: Wissenschaftliche Buchgesellschaft, 1990).—Trans.]

15. Plato, *Sophist,* 235d.

16. Ibid.

17. Ibid., 235e.

18. Ibid., 235e–236a.

19. Ibid., 236c.

20. [Plato's, Schleiermacher's, and White's terms thus align as follows: *mimesis eikastike—Ebenbildnerei—likeness-making* and *mimesis phantastike—Trugbildnerei—appearance-making.*—Trans.]

21. Gernot Böhme, *Theorie des Bildes* (Munich: Fink, 1999), 23.

22. Plato, *Sophist,* 236b. Alternatively, the term *non-appropriate* can be found instead of *appropriate* not only in the Greek manuscripts but even in the different editions of Schleiermacher's own translation. Schleiermacher's procedure, as can be seen from his own commentary, seems to have been the following: for reasons of content, Schleiermacher felt justified in deleting the Greek *ouk*, because that way, Plato's thought makes sense. We have to completely agree with Schleiermacher. A perspectival sculpture seems correctly proportioned from only one location; in this sense we can say that this location belongs to the sculpture. In short, "Thus, the *ouk* is to be deleted" (Schleiermacher, 501n). To support this content decision philologically, Schleiermacher can refer to Greek variants that do not include the *ouk* either: "finally, we have found some manuscripts that do the same" (ibid.). [White translates as "from a viewpoint that's not beautiful," thus not deleting the *ouk*.—Trans.]

23. Plato, *Sophist,* 236b.

24. Iris Därmann, "Mehr als ein Abbild / kein Abbild mehr: Derridas Bilder" [More Than a Picture / No Longer a Picture: Derrida's Images], *Phänomenologische Forschungen,* n.s. 1 (1996): 239–68, 251.

25. Heinrich Niehues-Pröbsting, *Überredung zur Einsicht: Der Zusammenhang von Philosophie und Rhetorik bei Platon und in der Phänomenologie* [Persuasion to Insight: The Relation of Philosophy and Rhetoric in Plato and in Phenomenology] (Frankfurt: Klostermann, 1987), 150.

26. Iris Därmann, *Tod und Bild: Eine phänomenologische Mediengeschichte* [Death and Image: A Phenomenological Media History] (Munich: Fink, 1995), 92.

CHAPTER 8

1. Boris Groys, *Unter Verdacht: Eine Phänomenologie der Medien* (Munich: Hanser, 2000).

2. Maurice Merleau-Ponty, *The Prose of the World*, ed. Claude Lefort, trans. John O'Neill (Evanston, IL: Northwestern University Press, 1973), 9–10.

3. See Maurice Merleau-Ponty, *The Visible and the Invisible*, ed. Claude Lefort, trans. Alphonso Lingis (Evanston, IL: Northwestern University Press, 1968), 30.

4. Christian Bermes, "Medialität—anthropologisches Radikal oder ontologisches Prinzip? Merleau-Pontys Ausführung der Phänomenologie" [Mediality—Anthropological Radical or Ontological Principle? Merleau-Ponty's Elaboration of Phenomenology], in *Die Stellung des Menschen in der Kultur: Festschrift für Ernst Wolfgang Orth*, ed. Christian Bermes, Julia Jonas, and Karl-Heinz Lembeck (Würzburg: Königshausen und Neumann, 2002), 41–58, 49.

5. Matthias Vogel, *Medien der Vernunft: Eine Theorie des Geistes und der Rationalität auf Grundlage einer Theorie der Medien* (Frankfurt: Suhrkamp, 2001), 13, 136, 133.

6. Georg Christoph Tholen, *Die Zäsur der Medien: Kulturphilosophische Konturen* (Frankfurt: Suhrkamp, 2002), 50, 8, 19.

7. Vogel, *Medien der Vernunft*, 144.

8. Edmund Husserl, *Logical Investigations*, trans. J. N. Findlay, ed. Dermot Moran (London: Routledge, 2001), pt. 1, chap. 8, § 46, 110.

9. Ibid.

10. Ibid., 109.

11. Ibid., pt. 1, chap. 7, § 36, 80.

12. [The distinction between *das gleiche* (what is equal, equivalent, or the same) and *dasselbe* (what is the same and identical with itself) can only insufficiently be rendered in English. The example in the next paragraph, however, will clarify the point.—Trans.]

13. Husserl, *Logical Investigations*, pt. 1, chap. 7, § 36, 80.

14. Ibid., pt. 1, chap. 8, § 46, 109.

15. Lorenz Engell and Joseph Vogl, "Vorwort," in *Kursbuch Medienkultur: Die maßgeblichen Theorien von Brecht bis Baudrillard*, ed. Claus Pias, Joseph Vogl, Lorenz Engell, Oliver Fahle, and Britta Neitzel (Stuttgart: DVA, 1999), 8–11, 10.

16. Hans Jonas, "Homo pictor and the Differentia of Man," *Social Research* 29, no. 2 (summer 1962): 201–20, 207.

17. Husserl, *Logical Investigations*, pt. 1, 5th Investigation, supplement to §§ 11 and 20, 126 [entirely retranslated].

Glossary

appearance	*Erscheinung*: the coming into appearance of something; *Aussehen*: the way something looks
assimilation	*Angleichung*: *gleichen* can mean "to be similar to," hence *angleichen*: to assimilate
attendance	*Anwesenheit*
copy	*Imitation*, compare "imitation"
denotatum	*Denotat, Bezeichnetes*: the signified
depiction	*Darstellung, bildliche Darstellung*
image	*Bild*; but note "to picture" for *abbilden* and "pictoriality" for *Bildlichkeit*; compare "image carrier," "image object," and "image subject"
image, figurative	*Abbild*: an image of a discernible object, as opposed to an abstract image
image carrier	*Bildträger*: the material support of an image (e.g., a canvas)
image object	*Bildobjekt*: what is visible on the image carrier and can be seen by the observer; the intentional object of the observer (e.g., the tree on the canvas)
image studies	*Bildwissenschaft*: the empirical and historical study of images of any kind
image subject	*Bildsujet*: what the image pictures, what the image object refers to (e.g., the real tree)

image theory	*Bildtheorie*: a part of philosophy, thus to be equated with a philosophy of the image
imitation	*Nachahmung*, includes both depictions and copies, or replicas
perception, approach based on	*wahrnehmungstheoretischer Ansatz:* a theoretical approach based on philosophical accounts of perception
pictoriality	*Bildlichkeit*: the quality that makes an image an image
presence	*Gegenwart, Präsenz*, to be distinguished from the purely temporal present, which is also *Gegenwart*
presentness	*Gegenwärtigkeit*

Cultural Memory | in the Present

Richard Rorty and Eduardo Mendieta, *Take Care of Freedom and Truth Will Take Care of Itself: Interviews with Richard Rorty*

Jacques Derrida, *Paper Machine*

Renaud Barbaras, *Desire and Distance: Introduction to a Phenomenology of Perception*

Jill Bennett, *Empathic Vision: Affect, Trauma, and Contemporary Art*

Ban Wang, *Illuminations from the Past: Trauma, Memory, and History in Modern China*

James Phillips, *Heidegger's Volk: Between National Socialism and Poetry*

Frank Ankersmit, *Sublime Historical Experience*

István Rév, *Retroactive Justice: Prehistory of Post-Communism*

Paola Marrati, *Genesis and Trace: Derrida Reading Husserl and Heidegger*

Krzysztof Ziarek, *The Force of Art*

Marie-José Mondzain, *Image, Icon, Economy: The Byzantine Origins of the Contemporary Imaginary*

Cecilia Sjöholm, *The Antigone Complex: Ethics and the Invention of Feminine Desire*

Jacques Derrida and Elisabeth Roudinesco, *For What Tomorrow . . . : A Dialogue*

Elisabeth Weber, *Questioning Judaism: Interviews by Elisabeth Weber*

Jacques Derrida and Catherine Malabou, *Counterpath: Traveling with Jacques Derrida*

Martin Seel, *Aesthetics of Appearing*

Nanette Salomon, *Shifting Priorities: Gender and Genre in Seventeenth-Century Dutch Painting*

Jacob Taubes, *The Political Theology of Paul*

Jean-Luc Marion, *The Crossing of the Visible*

Eric Michaud, *An Art for Eternity: The Cult of Art in Nazi Germany*

Anne Freadman, *The Machinery of Talk: Charles Peirce and the Sign Hypothesis*

Stanley Cavell, *Emerson's Transcendental Etudes*

Stuart McLean, *The Event and Its Terrors: Ireland, Famine, Modernity*

Beate Rössler, ed., *Privacies: Philosophical Evaluations*

Bernard Faure, *Double Exposure: Cutting Across Buddhist and Western Discourses*

Alessia Ricciardi, *The Ends of Mourning: Psychoanalysis, Literature, Film*

Alain Badiou, *Saint Paul: The Foundation of Universalism*

Gil Anidjar, *The Jew, The Arab: A History of the Enemy*

Jonathan Culler and Kevin Lamb, eds., *Just Being Difficult? Academic Writing in the Public Arena*

Jean-Luc Nancy, *A Finite Thinking*, edited by Simon Sparks

Theodor W. Adorno, *Can One Live after Auschwitz? A Philosophical Reader*, edited by Rolf Tiedemann

Patricia Pisters, *The Matrix of Visual Culture: Working with Deleuze in Film Theory*

Talal Asad, *Formations of the Secular: Christianity, Islam, Modernity*

Dorothea von Mücke, *The Rise of the Fantastic Tale*

Marc Redfield, *The Politics of Aesthetics: Nationalism, Gender, Romanticism*

Emmanuel Levinas, *On Escape*

Dan Zahavi, *Husserl's Phenomenology*

Rodolphe Gasché, *The Idea of Form: Rethinking Kant's Aesthetics*

Michael Naas, *Taking on the Tradition: Jacques Derrida and the Legacies of Deconstruction*

Herlinde Pauer-Studer, ed., *Constructions of Practical Reason: Interviews on Moral and Political Philosophy*

Jean-Luc Marion, *Being Given: Toward a Phenomenology of Givenness*

Theodor W. Adorno and Max Horkheimer, *Dialectic of Enlightenment*

Ian Balfour, *The Rhetoric of Romantic Prophecy*

Martin Stokhof, *World and Life as One: Ethics and Ontology in Wittgenstein's Early Thought*

Gianni Vattimo, *Nietzsche: An Introduction*

Jacques Derrida, *Negotiations: Interventions and Interviews, 1971–1998*, ed. Elizabeth Rottenberg

Brett Levinson, *The Ends of Literature: Post-transition and Neoliberalism in the Wake of the "Boom"*

Timothy J. Reiss, *Against Autonomy: Global Dialectics of Cultural Exchange*

Hent de Vries and Samuel Weber, eds., *Religion and Media*

Niklas Luhmann, *Theories of Distinction: Redescribing the Descriptions of Modernity*, ed. and introd. William Rasch

Johannes Fabian, *Anthropology with an Attitude: Critical Essays*

Michel Henry, *I Am the Truth: Toward a Philosophy of Christianity*

Gil Anidjar, *"Our Place in Al-Andalus": Kabbalah, Philosophy, Literature in Arab-Jewish Letters*

Hélène Cixous and Jacques Derrida, *Veils*

F. R. Ankersmit, *Historical Representation*

F. R. Ankersmit, *Political Representation*

Elissa Marder, *Dead Time: Temporal Disorders in the Wake of Modernity (Baudelaire and Flaubert)*

Reinhart Koselleck, *The Practice of Conceptual History: Timing History, Spacing Concepts*

Niklas Luhmann, *The Reality of the Mass Media*

Hubert Damisch, *A Childhood Memory by Piero della Francesca*

Hubert Damisch, *A Theory of /Cloud/: Toward a History of Painting*

Jean-Luc Nancy, *The Speculative Remark (One of Hegel's Bons Mots)*

Jean-François Lyotard, *Soundproof Room: Malraux's Anti-Aesthetics*

Jan Patočka, *Plato and Europe*

Hubert Damisch, *Skyline: The Narcissistic City*

Isabel Hoving, *In Praise of New Travelers: Reading Caribbean Migrant Women Writers*

Richard Rand, ed., *Futures: Of Derrida*

William Rasch, *Niklas Luhmann's Modernity: The Paradox of System Differentiation*

Jacques Derrida and Anne Dufourmantelle, *Of Hospitality*

Jean-François Lyotard, *The Confession of Augustine*

Kaja Silverman, *World Spectators*

Samuel Weber, *Institution and Interpretation: Expanded Edition*

Jeffrey S. Librett, *The Rhetoric of Cultural Dialogue: Jews and Germans in the Epoch of Emancipation*

Ulrich Baer, *Remnants of Song: Trauma and the Experience of Modernity in Charles Baudelaire and Paul Celan*

Samuel C. Wheeler III, *Deconstruction as Analytic Philosophy*

David S. Ferris, *Silent Urns: Romanticism, Hellenism, Modernity*

Rodolphe Gasché, *Of Minimal Things: Studies on the Notion of Relation*

Sarah Winter, *Freud and the Institution of Psychoanalytic Knowledge*

Samuel Weber, *The Legend of Freud: Expanded Edition*

Aris Fioretos, ed., *The Solid Letter: Readings of Friedrich Hölderlin*

J. Hillis Miller / Manuel Asensi, *Black Holes / J. Hillis Miller; or, Boustrophedonic Reading*

Miryam Sas, *Fault Lines: Cultural Memory and Japanese Surrealism*

Peter Schwenger, *Fantasm and Fiction: On Textual Envisioning*

Didier Maleuvre, *Museum Memories: History, Technology, Art*

Jacques Derrida, *Monolingualism of the Other; or, The Prosthesis of Origin*

Andrew Baruch Wachtel, *Making a Nation, Breaking a Nation: Literature and Cultural Politics in Yugoslavia*

Niklas Luhmann, *Love as Passion: The Codification of Intimacy*

Mieke Bal, ed., *The Practice of Cultural Analysis: Exposing Interdisciplinary Interpretation*

Jacques Derrida and Gianni Vattimo, eds., *Religion*